A Magpie Life

Also by George Bowering

A

#

L I F E

Growing a Writer

George Bowering

KEY PORTER 〜 **BOOKS**

Canadian Cataloguing in Publication Data

Bowering, George, 1935-
  A magpie life

Includes index.
ISBN 1-55263-348-9

1. Bowering, George, 1935- . 2. Authors, Canadian (English) – 20th century – Biography.* I. Title.

PS8503.O875Z53 2001   C818'.5409   C00-933326-6
PR9199.3.B63Z47 2001

The Canada Council | Le Conseil des Arts
for the arts | du Canada
since 1957 | depuis 1957

The publisher gratefully acknowledges the assistance of the Canada Council and the Ontario Arts Council.

We acknowledge the financial support of the Government of Canada through the Book Publishing Industry Development Program (BPIDP) for our publishing activities.

The excerpt on page 27 is from Charles Olson's "The Kingfishers" copyright the Estate of Charles Olson and the University of Connecticut. Used with permission; the excerpt on page 151 is from the *The Dangerous Summer* by Ernest Hemingway. Copyright © 1960 by Ernest Hemingway. Copyright renewed © 1988 by John Hemingway, Patrick Hemingway, and Gregory Hemingway. Excerpt used by permission of Scribner, a Division of Simon & Schuster, Inc.; the excerpt on page 213 is from Al Purdy's "Love at Roblin Lake" from *Beyond Remembering*, Harbour Publishing, 2000. Used with permission.

Key Porter Books Limited
70 The Esplanade
Toronto, Ontario
Canada M5E 1R2
www.keyporter.com

Electronic formatting: Jean Lightfoot Peters
Design: Peter Maher

01 02 03 04 05 6 5 4 3 2 1

This is for

𝓐𝓑,

WHO WAS THERE FROM THE BEGINNING.

Some parts of this book were published, in earlier versions, in the following:

Arts Vancouver, Books in Canada, Brick, The Canadian Broadcasting Corporation, Canadian Literature, Canadian Poetry, The Capilano Review, Contemporary Authors, Elysian Fields Quarterly, Essays in Canadian Writing, The Globe and Mail, In 2 Print, Minutes of the Charles Olson Society, Open Letter, Queen Street Quarterly, La questione romantica, Sagetrieb, The Vancouver Review.

"The Ryerson Split" was published in The Rain Barrel, Talonbooks, 1994. "Parashoot!" was published in Fresh Tracks: writing the western landscape, ed. Pamela Banting, Polestar Books, 1998.

CONTENTS

ALPHABIOGRAPHY

Alphabiography

NGELA LUOMA AND I got married at Vancouver city hall on December 14, 1962. We were living in a very old apartment building on Yew Street with a hill outside that was steep enough to park my 1954 Austin on, so that it would start if you got it rolling. Today, in the light rain, it would not start for several blocks, and Angela Luoma was waiting at the hairdresser's, speaking of me with impolite language. The hairdresser was necessary. He was trying to get her hair all one colour of blonde because the hairdressing student had made it three colours the day before.

We were fifteen minutes late at city hall, but Angela was used to this, because it was her way, and now more than half a life later, though I saw that it seemed to work for her, I was still not used to it. I would have liked to be at city hall a half-hour early, in my black hopsack jacket and narrow bebop tie, and now when Angela was not with me I always got there early. When we were together, we would arrive after something had already started. I hope, I said, she would get to my funeral before it's over.

She was beautiful with her blonde hair and green eyes and we were married before my first book was published, when I had published a few poems in the magazines. I was a graduate student at the University of British Columbia, where I was helping to publish an international poetry newsletter called *Tish*, with Frank Davey and Fred Wah and some other young poets. Robert Duncan encouraged us to start the mag, and gave it its title. First Fred got married to Pauline Butling, then I got married to Angela, and then Frank got married to Helen.

Angela Luoma was half Finnish and half Anglo-Scottish. She had read everything that I had not read—Plato and Tolstoy and Jung.

She was interested in gardens and psychology and mortgages and genealogy. She was not a poet, and she did not often write anything beyond her stacks of personal journals, but she published a book on Sheila Watson's wonderful novel *The Double Hook*. She was an expert on Sheila Watson. That was the part of her that I liked best.

Angela Bowering had a short fuse, and I did not play with matches around her. I liked her large green eyes, but I would never strike a match to make the pupils dilate.

IRTH WAS SOMETHING I have been trying to get over all my life. My mother, Pearl, gave birth to me, her first child, in Penticton, B.C., at 11:30 P.M. on December 1, 1935. She was nineteen years old, it was the middle of the Depression, and her schoolteacher husband received ninety dollars a month, or nothing at all if the school district could not manage it.

It took more than two days for her to manage it, November slipping away, her husband Ewart trudging up the hill to the Penticton hospital whenever his fellow bridge players would let him. I came into the world, such as it was, sideways. My enormous head was black and all mushy, they say, and my mother tried to resolve herself to the likelihood that after they took the baby away somewhere she might not see it again, or that it would have no appreciable brain. Still, she and her husband gave it a name. The name had been Richard for six months, but now they did not want to run the risk of wasting that name. They called me George Harry Bowering, after my father Ewart Harry Bowering and his English immigrant father Jabez Harry Bowering. If this baby were to live, the Penticton hospital said, the damage to its head would likely demand their patience in the coming years.

They worked all through the day, Dr. McGregor, Miss Riley, Miss Miller, Miss Dawson. The sideways thing with the bleeding head was only seven pounds and fourteen ounces. Average. In the baby book, under remarks: "?"

A question mark. Looking at that page all these years later, I bless the hand that wrote it. My father, according to the family joke, was playing bridge with their friends down the hill when the awkward flesh began its journey to death or maybe life in the Okanagan Valley. But then there he was and there I was and maybe he could see me soon. Pearl was a year and a half out of school where they lived in Peachland.

When they let us leave she was back in her polka-dot dress and a coat to cover her bare arms, at the end of the year in the very centre of the Depression. She was full of milk and looking forward to the summer when she could get back onto the ball field. When his head was better, someone else could hold him for a little.

CHILDHOOD IS THOUGHT, by people better read than I am, to be a powerful determinant of one's later life. It could be. A lot of people look back on their childhood as an Edenic time, filled with innocence and clean air. I grew up in the Okanagan Valley. It was gouged out in the ice age, became a semi-desert and a string of lakes. When I was a child it was a couple hundred miles of orchard, blossoms in the spring, heavy fruit all summer, from the cherries in June to the apples of September.

The hills were dry and looked just like the landscape in western movies. Children hiked around those hills all year round, looking out in summer for cactuses and rattlesnakes, in winter for a frozen pond to stomp on. In elementary school they instructed us on what to do in case of a rattlesnake bite. We sometimes heard about tourists getting bitten, but I never knew anyone who got bitten by a rattler. We would acquire their rattles and then sneak up behind someone and shake them. I have jumped a mile.

When we lived in Oliver, where my father was a science

teacher, we had Bowering relatives up the valley, in Summerland and Penticton and Naramata, and Brinson relatives over in the Kootenays. We were always visiting the Bowering relatives, and I loved it. In the Okanagan Valley I had only one cousin older than I, Russell Bowering the jazz saxophone player, and he died when I was a kid. So I managed to develop that solitariness the oldest kid learns about. It leads you to such things as books and California radio stations, and the peculiarities of Okanagan geology.

For most of my childhood I had a dog, and this was back when there was open space right in town. A dog could crap wherever he wanted to, except on Mrs. Wilkins's lawn. First I had Caesar, and I dont remember what happened to him. Then I had Caesar the Second, a wire-haired terrier. He always fought ferociously with my uncle Red's wire-haired terrier named Beans. We left him tied in the orchard when I was in grade three, and when we came back he was gone. Then there was the cocker spaniel Monty. When we moved into town we sent him to the orchard where my uncle Gerry lived, and Monty got run over by a tractor. Then there was Dinky, an English rat terrier with a big-letter *S* scar on her back. I inherited her when my grandmother Brinson died. Dinky was my favourite. She took twenty million steps in the hills over Oliver.

*D*EATH ALWAYS BOTHERED me more than birth did. When I was four I thought I could get older till I was very old and then get younger a year at a time. You would have to pick your friends carefully, in case they might be coming down when you were going up. When I was five I thought I might be the first person in modern times to live forever. When I was six I thought I could start as someone else after I died, with no memory.

When I was sixteen I thought I would die before I was thirty. When I was twenty-nine I had been married for two years. I lived with my widow in Calgary. My unlucky number has been fifty-two ever since I was a child. Several of my books go directly from chapter fifty-one to chapter fifty-three. I wondered whether I would end in my fifty-second year or when I was fifty-two. I was living with my wife and orphaned daughter in Vancouver. Years ago people used to wonder what political life would be like in 1984. We found out that books are just books.

Death is one of the very biggest subjects of poetry. I have been writing about it all my life. I usually try to show a humorous side to the subject. My 1992 book *Urban Snow* includes a funny poem called "Death." The publisher demurred when I told him I wanted to call the book *Death and Other Poems*. It seems to me that as I have grown older we have enjoyed more nice machines in our houses while watching our particular world dying. In the Okanagan Valley there are more and more stumps where there used to be peach trees, and new houses with paved driveways where there used to be sagebrush hills that looked like western movies.

After my cousin Russell died, my grandmother Bowering died. The only time I ever saw my father weep was at her funeral in the Baptist church in Summerland. I was fascinated by the beauty of a young woman in the choir, and I felt that I was an awful human being because I did not cry at all. When I was in elementary school the news came that Tom Moojalski's father had been killed by a log falling off a truck. When I was in junior high school my classmate Tibor Palley died in the Oliver hospital while telling Jesus that he loved him.

On my twenty-ninth birthday I got the news by telephone and telegram that my best friend Red Lane had died in Vancouver. He was just starting to be a poet.

EWART BOWERING WAS just my father, and he died on March 12, 1975. His funeral was held at the United church in Oliver, on the Ides of March. I held my mother's hand and my sister's hand, hard. We were in the front row, privileged and vulnerable. I thought I heard his voice saying "It's all right."

He was just my father, but now I have come to know and to admit that he is a kind of hero to me, a standard against which I measure my behaviour. When I was younger I maintained this story—that he was a very smart and promising man who settled for less because it was the Depression. He was smarter than all his brothers and sisters but he always got along with them well, playing bridge, working summers in the orchard.

He was a preacher's son and an athlete. I have his small-town newspaper clippings in which he is usually the best player in the basketball game, or he got two singles in the baseball game. I have his first school inspector's reports, in which he is praised for his dedication and chided for his shortcomings as a disciplinarian. He had blue eyes and a straight nose. He was just about six feet tall and handsome. My mother was a schoolgirl athlete from a hillbilly family and she snagged him.

He was a quiet man who paid a lot of attention to his community. He coached young people's basketball teams and softball teams. He was secretary-treasurer of the Elks Club but he seldom had a drink; he organized their Save the Children fund. He worked on the committee to get the new hospital in Oliver. He started the fire every morning. He never drove over the speed limit. He wrote sports reports for the small-town newspapers when he got to be too old to be in them. He took off his shirt and in his undershirt built our house. He didnt like it when people said "nucular" or made plurals out of apostrophes.

He was the chemistry teacher at Southern Okanagan High School. I had to take a senior science course to graduate, so I took chemistry. I got 56 per cent in chemistry. At school I called him Sir and he called me Bowering. After his funeral we went to the desert cemetery up Fairview Road in

Oliver, and I broke away from the cluster of family and put my lips to his casket. I was surprised at myself.

*F*IRST TIMES AT THINGS are supposed to be memorable, and some are, though they will be fictionalized or made lyric by the memory. At the time they are part of a continuum, confused with everything else that is happening that day in that body and mind. Is this the first time I have written autobiography? Well, yes and well, no.

We do a hundred thousand things for the first time, and really one can argue that everything we do we are doing for the first time. The game of baseball is so damned beautiful because so familiar. We knew that Devon White would lead off and reach base, and then Roberto Alomar would hit in the second spot, for instance, just as Billy Herman followed Peewee Reese. The first time I ever came to bat in organized junior baseball I hit a single with the bases loaded. Shortly after that I had to move out of town, to work in the orchard in Naramata.

Three important firsts are in baseball, sex, and writing. My first honest-to-God, all-the-way sexual initiation occurred one afternoon in Portage la Prairie, Manitoba. My guide, though I still like to think she didnt know, was a farmer's daughter named Eileen, who was a wonderful one year older than I. In all probability I was finished awfully early, and because I was in the air force my dog tags clinked on her teeth. I didnt know whether it was all right to think things were funny while you were doing it. Thank you, Eileen.

There are a lot of little writing firsts, arent there? Poems in school magazines, a letter published in *Baseball Digest*, a story in an anthology in Toronto. My first real book, *Points on the Grid*, made me happy in a sense. I was in my late twenties, and full of myself, a big fan of Charles Olson, and now I had a book of poems published by Contact Press, the best small press for the new poetry in Canada. Of course we were living in Calgary, where no one, including the people who taught poetry at the university, knew anything about the world I had taken my first step into.

A few years ago a copy of that book was sold for fifteen hundred dollars. The poetry in it isnt very good. But this isnt the first time one has perceived the real relationship between art and commodity.

*G*EORGE WAS NOT SUPPOSED to be my name, but at the last minute that is what they gave me. I've never been satisfied with it. When I have to tell an answering service who it is that's calling, I'm a little embarrassed to say the word. My mother once told me how neat it is that all the letters of my first name also show up in my last name. The same can be said for my kid brother Roger. And when I see my name on the cover of a book, for instance, I like the way that only the capitals stick up above the rest, and the *g*s stick down. I'm glad my name isnt Elroy Holmquist.

But when I was a boy I thought I'd like the name Ted. Theodore. My aunt Dorothy died shortly after I was born. She was a nurse in a meningitis hospital, and died of the same thing Thomas Wolfe died of, in the same year. They were both fatally sick in British Columbia. The next year Theodore Samuel Williams arrived in the American League. He was to become my favourite ballplayer.

Maybe if I had been born Richard or Theodore, I wouldnt have tried to make a name for myself.

The only other George in my family is my mother's uncle George, who was some kind of gambler and later crank religion pamphleteer in Louisiana. He and his siblings all came up to Canada from the Ozarks to be hillbillies on the Prairies. He married his brother Emmett's wife's sister, and headed back south. The last I heard of him he was in Georgia. I've never been there.

But the Bowerings got here when my other grandfather, Jabez Harry, came as an orphaned boy to be an indentured farm labourer. He got smart or religion, and became a circuit rider on the Prairies. By the time I knew him he shuffled with a crutch and a cane, and was the postmaster at Summerland. Once he showed me a thousand-dollar bill. When he got old and moved from Summerland to Penticton he took his furnace with him. After his wife Clara died he moved in with us in Oliver. My father being the way he was, naturally it was to our house that Grandpa came. My father built some more of our house.

I guess the name George is all right for writers as long as they are writers. I have always liked the work of George Oppen, George Stanley, George Economou, and Georgia Savage. People who have read more than I have tell me that Lord Byron is pretty good.

HOME IS VERY IMPORTANT to me, I have found out to my surprise in various self-examination exercises. I have been living in the same house now for twenty-five years, which is a bit shocking, because when I was younger I thought that I would keep on moving every year from house to house, every couple of years to another town. But when you live in Vancouver at last, do you want to live in another town?

I have lived in thirty houses and apartments, not counting temporary shelters like tents, bunkhouses, borrowed houses, barracks, dormitories, and hotels. Before I left my parents' home at age seventeen, I lived in Summerland, Greenwood, and Oliver. Then I went for a year of college in Victoria. I was in the Royal Canadian Air Force as a photographer for three years, living in Ontario, Quebec, and Manitoba except for temporary duty elsewhere. After that I became a student again, at the University of British Columbia, and I strung that out as long as I could, living in a basement here, a loft there.

So we got married, Angela Luoma and I, in December of 1962, and in 1963 I got a teaching job in Calgary, where we lived in three apartments, going to Mexico for a while in the summers. One of our addresses in Mexico was on Calle Béisbol. In 1966, after my first summer in Europe, we went to London, Ontario for a year, where I did course work for my Ph.D. and Angela worked in a psychology laboratory where they put pigeon brains in other pigeons. Then we went to Montreal where I could be a writer in residence at Sir George Williams University, and we stayed for almost four years. They expected me back in Calgary. They expected me back in London.

Instead I quit my job again and we headed for the West Coast. I wrote some books and we had a baby, Thea Bowering, in 1971, and a year later I landed a job at Simon Fraser University. Every time I get a job, it is by the skin of my teeth.

When our daughter was born we were living in a commune on York Avenue. A little later we finally bought a little house on Balaclava Street, so there was one of my rules, broken. Then, twenty-five years ago, we bought a big old house on Thirty-seventh Avenue, and that is where the three of us stayed ever after, except for the year I was writer in residence in Rome and Berlin.

I dont hang my hat. I put it on a shelf.

J NDIANS AND BASEBALL, that's what W. P. Kinsella writes about, and come to think of it, that's what I write about. Come to think of it, the last time I saw W. P. Kinsella we were in Cleveland Stadium, watching the Indians play baseball quite well against the White Sox.

When I was a kid in western-movie Oliver, the Wenatchee Chiefs professional baseball team held their spring training at our park. Manuel Louie, the chief of the local band, would let the fake Chiefs use his sweat house in exchange for letting him take batting practice. He was always old, Manuel Louie, and everyone loved him. He wore a big round Stetson hat with an eagle feather in it, and placed his powerful belly over the rail of the snooker table back of the Orchard Cafe. He was old and fit, and I thought of him and the pictures of Honus Wagner in my baseball magazines. They were both bow-legged and old and perfectly qualified to be legends.

My novel *Caprice* is dedicated to Manuel Louie and Windy Bone. *Caprice* is about Indians and baseball. Windy Bone told me "The Indian Way to Catch a Deer," and it is funny as hell. I sat in the Desert Arms pub, which used to be the Reopel Hotel beer parlour, and had a beer while Windy had a Coke. I said there are white professors who say "native," or "indigene," or "First Nation" instead of "Indian." Windy thought that was funny as hell.

The difference between the West and the East is that if you're a white guy growing up in the West, you work with Indian guys, and if you shoot pool, you lose snooker games to Indian guys. In the East, if you're a white guy, you hardly ever see Indian guys, or Indian people at all, except on the television news.

So poetry and fiction. In Canada, poetry and fiction in the East dont have Indians in them any more. But look at western Canadian fiction. It's like growing up in Western Canada. Indians fill up books by Robert Kroetsch, Sheila Watson, Rudy Wiebe, Susan Musgrave, W. P. Kinsella, and me. Now look around some more. Jeanette Armstrong, the Okanagan Indian writer, is from Penticton. The first novel written by an Indian woman, Mourning Dove, also came from the Okanagan. Keep an eye out for Lee Maracle and J. B. Joe. All women, all Indian, native women, if you like. I dont think any of them play baseball, though.

*J*OURNEYING IS NOT the opposite of home; it is the partner—my friend bp Nichol's first book of poetry was called *Journeying and the Returns*. Coming home is part of the journey, that means, and it suggests that travel is always going on, while getting home is plural. I wrote a novel about that, *Harry's Fragments*.

When I was a kid in the Okanagan Valley, I did not live in a family that travelled. My father never got off this continent, and only once in his life went as far east as Montreal. I took him to see a game between the Expos and the St. Louis Cardinals. When I was a kid in the Okanagan, I sometimes went to other towns up the valley. Kelowna, for instance, was sixty miles away. It was pretty romantic: you had to take a ferry across the lake to get to Kelowna, until they built the bridge.

By her twentieth birthday, my daughter had been to Europe four times. I first got to Europe in the summer of 1966, when I was thirty. My friend Tony Bellette went to Germany to buy a Volkswagen, and I went with him. We rode from England to Turkey and back in the bug, and my budget was six dollars a day. I took my portable typewriter and wrote a book about the trip, fifteen hundred words a day for six weeks. I also kept my diary, and wrote home every day.

Since then I have been to Europe fairly often. It's my favourite foreign destination, as they say. I go to all the cathedrals and all the art museums. I have never been to a nightclub. People who like to know favourites will hear that my favourite cathedral is the white Romanesque marble one in Pisa, and my favourite art museum, well, I keep changing my mind. Lately it's been the Prado.

I have been to the Antipodes five or six times, and I have been to some art museums there, but I dont often go into churches in Australia or New Zealand. I went to the humble clay-like cathedral in Papeete once. I felt like Paul Gauguin.

My favourite city in the world is Trieste. When I was ready to write my novel *Burning Water* I had the excitement and luxury of choosing a place to write it. Having been through Trieste with Tony Bellette in 1966, I chose that old James Joyce Hapsburg spy city of white mountains, red roofs, and blue sea. Since then I have found a way to work

Trieste into most of my other books and the autobiography of one of my pen names.

KEROUAC HAD TO BE A watermark for me. For some reason I have always been fond of books by writers whose names start with *K*. Often I am connected with them. When I was a new poet down out of the mountains and looking around for my kith and kin at the University of British Columbia, the first guy I hooked up with was Lionel Kearns, who had come down out of the mountains just east of mine, i.e., the Kootenays. We learned and stole a lot from each other. My first book, *Sticks & Stones*, is dedicated to Lionel Kearns.

Lionel introduced me to the writing of Jack Kerouac, who made my blood sing and my sentences zip. I gobbled his books up. I'm still playing tapes of Kerouac in my Volvo.

My second book, *The Man in Yellow Boots*, was published bilingually in Mexico, the year in which Lionel Kearns stayed at our house on Calle Béisbol. It contains collages by Roy Kiyooka. It also contains, in both languages, a poem by Roy. I've long been glad of my association with Kiyooka, and I've written several essays about his painting, sculpture, and poetry.

I have never read a book by Franz Kafka. But I have quoted, translated, and plagiarized John Keats for years. Joy Kogawa and W. P. Kinsella were born the year I was born, though earlier, I always remind myself, in the year. I get along with both of them, but I am a little more likely to read Milan Kundera or Ivan Klima.

I always say that the best writer in Canada is Robert Kroetsch. I suppose that I ought not to say the best this and my favourite that. But when I first read Kroetsch's fiction it was with that rare coupling of feelings—the prose was a delight to read, and its formal ideas spoke their importance confidently. You can get that double whammo from Italo Calvino or William H. Gass.

Kroetsch has, for three decades, also written wonderful eccentric essays, reaching postmodern European discourse theory, and standing on western Canadian tricksterism. Usually the best novelists and essayists are busts when they dare to write poetry. But Kroetsch set his hand and wonky head to poetry and changed the world for some of Canada's best poets.

He also married a young Greek woman who was to become a fiction writer and major avant-garde critic. Her name is, of course, Kamboureli.

*L*ITERATURE GOT ME when my guard was lowered by books. Since I was fourteen years old, or was it twelve, I have been writing in scribblers the titles and authors and publishers of all the books I read, and keeping track of the number of books I have read by each author. I have read eighteen books by Fielding Dawson. I have read thirty-five books by Robert Creeley.

In the first scribbler the books are often by Max Brand and Robert Heinlein. In the second scribbler they are often by James M. Cain and James T. Farrell. You see how it was going. In the most recent scribbler they are by Nathalie Sarraute and Adolfo Bioy Casares. First I read books, and as I got older I read literature.

I have often said that growing up with some loneliness and intelligence in a semi-desert village led to my being a writer. What can you do after reading a lot of books other than to write some? In Oliver there was really no painting, no sculpture, no ballet, no symphony. There was amateur drama, especially at school, so I acted in a lot of plays. There was *Life* magazine, and my pal Bill Lyttle and I had a darkroom under his basement stairs. And there was the bus depot candy store across from the movie theatre. It had baseball magazines and mass-market paperbacks.

I wanted, mainly, to be a baseball writer, so I wrote

baseball for the weekly Oliver *Chronicle* and the daily Penticton *Herald*. I got paid ten cents a column inch. And I guess I wanted to write mass-market paperbacks. Years later I wrote a swashbuckling sea story called *Burning Water*, a western called *Caprice*, and an international spy novel called *Harry's Fragments*. But by then literature had got hold of me. *Burning Water* is a reflexive fiction about a novelist's voyages, *Caprice* is an anti-western, or what the postmodern critic Linda Hutcheon calls a "historiographic metafiction," and *Harry's Fragments* is a narrative translation of Heraclitus. I have also written two novels of teenage science fiction. Genre precedes literature, and is its victim.

My mother Pearl still lives in Oliver. She reads books to relax, to pass the afternoon, to get ready for sleep. I travel around a lot and all I bring home is literature.

MONTREAL, FOR WRITERS of my generation, was mysterious, glamorous, foreign, big, old, and reputed to be terrific for jazz and vice and other nightlife. I was first there as a teenage air force recruit on weekend leave, and I got drunk because of Montreal's unpuritanical streets, and saluted the epauletted doorman in front of the Ritz-Carlton Hotel.

For young Canadian writers, Montreal had a reputation as the place where new poetry movements started, in French or English. For me, the origins of Contact Press, for instance, had been in the 1940s and 1950s literary magazines and manifestos of Irving Layton and Louis Dudek and Torontonian Raymond Souster. The English-language poetry scene in Montreal 1940–1965 has left us a record of great squabbles and momentous inventions. I became aware of all that ferment when Lionel Kearns showed me the small-press magazines and books he had brought home to UBC from his summer in Montreal. This must have been about 1959.

In 1967, Angela Bowering and I moved to Montreal. It was

the year of Canada's centenary and Expo '67 in Montreal. The city was full of U.S. Americans and others. There were two apartments available on what the locals call the west side of Montreal. One was over a Greek cafe on Greene Avenue. The other was on Grosvenor, just off the main drag of Sherbrooke Street. We lived in that long narrow flat for nearly four years, the longest we had lived anywhere by a long shot.

Pretty Exciting. I was thirty-one years old and a writer in residence. I met all the Montreal poets, who stood around and talked about the old days when the young Marxists and the young aesthetes clashed. There was a new subway. The buildings were made of stone, long ago. I started to buy inexpensive velvet clothes. Friends from the rest of Canada and the U.S. slept all over our apartment. It was the big city. In a couple of years the Montreal Expos and the National League arrived. You could get to New York on the train. Really young poets came to see me and I told them about Jack Spicer and Frank O'Hara, and in some cases it stuck.

But I didnt write much about Montreal. One very short story got finished. A thin volume of poems occurred a few years later, nothing to write home about. It was while we lived in Montreal that I got into the habit of writing long poems instead of lyrics about my surroundings. I have been writing long poems longer and longer ever since.

*N*ORTH IS SUPPOSED to be an important concept for Canadians, maybe the way West was for U.S. Americans. North is supposed to be mystical, national, psychological. During the heyday of thematic criticism in the post-centenary 1970s we often heard of the Northern Experience, something we Canadians were supposed to share with Scandinavians, I think.

But I grew up in a desert valley, where the temperature often went over a hundred, back when we used impressive Fahrenheit degrees. I went on to live in Alberta and

Manitoba, in Ontario and Quebec, but I never learned to have fun in the snow. Nowadays I live in the southwest corner of the country and make flying visits to snow country, to do a reading in Montreal, say, or Edmonton. I revel in the experience of a "Canadian winter" for a few days, pull my toque down off the shelf and over my moussed hair, knowing I'll be back out of the blizzard next week.

The Australians have a similar myth. Where we have the North, they have the outback, and its apotheosis, Ayre's Rock, is in the middle of the country, of that continent. But most Australians have never been to the outback; most of them travel by air from city to city on the coast. So it is in Canada, with our great myth. Most Canadians have never been to the North.

For one thing, it is very expensive to get up north. It helps to be a civil servant or petrochemical expert, so someone else will pay your way. It helps to be a Canadian writer. As a Canadian writer I have been to the Yukon twice, during the annual spring book festival. The first time I was there an outdoor-loving schoolteacher named Joyce Sward fed us some moose meat she had been keeping in the freezer. I thought nothing could be better. Then next time I was there she fed us some caribou. It was just the best meat I've ever eaten.

One August I did a reading tour that started right at the top of continental Canada, in Inuvik, and wended southward to Fort Smith, Northwest Territories. I did not do what a lot of Canadian poets would do—I did not write poems about the journey. But I will say something about it now: I cannot give you words about the North. I just wish I could go back, in the winter.

OLSONITES, WE JOKINGLY called ourselves. Olsonite was the brand name for a toilet seat, but we were confident enough about where we stood. We were a crew of young poets around 1961, who created what Canadian literature professors would call the Tish Movement. As far as we could see, Charles Olson was the main U.S. American poet, as Pound and Williams had been before him.

Olson told us to dig exhaustively into our local concerns. We began to do so, and the geography, history, and economics of Vancouver became the grid of our poetry. In the late 1960s and the 1970s, xenophobic critics and professors in Ontario accused us of selling out the "Canadian Tradition" to U.S. American interests. The latter would include Charles Olson and the anti-Vietnamese war machine. They started calling us Black Mountain poets. I dont know any Canadian poets who ever went to North Carolina. Once a typically poorly informed eastern professor asked me where in Vancouver Black Mountain might be. I was quizzical and tired. I said Black Mountain was just a few kilometres north of the city. To my surprise I found out years later that there is a ski hill called Black Mountain right there.

This is true: Charles Olson, Robert Duncan, Denise Levertov, and Robert Creeley were important to us. They were the previous generation. We were amazed to learn that while these poets constituted U.S. American poetry as far as we were concerned, they were still being marginalized in the U.S. Some visiting professor would start talking about Anthony Hecht or John Berryman, and we would be amazed.

> [B]ut under these petals
> in the emptiness
> regard the light, contemplate
> the flower
>
> whence it arose

—said Olson. He told us, with that demonstrative, what Heraclitus told us around the same time, to attend our own particulars, and if you will listen, to attend sometimes with simple beautiful song. That is, speak those words aloud. When Pound said that form is the test of a poet's sincerity, he was, demonstrably, right.

Some of us went to Buffalo, say, to study with Olson. I studied with Creeley in Vancouver. We are older than they were in 1961, but they are the history of the New World for us.

*P*ROSE OR POETRY, PHOTOGRAPHY, plays? Probably more than any others, Canadian writers work in more than one category. The more restive, such as Daphne Marlatt and Michael Ondaatje, like to transgress the apparent boundaries between fiction and poetry, say, or autobiography and novel. Others such as Margaret Atwood and Robert Kroetsch keep parallel careers (poet, novelist) going.

First I wanted to be a sports reporter. I wanted to be a baseball writer for the St. Louis *Post-Dispatch*, like Bob Broeg. Reporters are reputed to keep their secret and unsuccessful novels in their desk drawers, along with the flask of whisky. I've always been a closet sports journalist (and jazz writer). In Montreal I wrote sports for a short-lived community arts and politics magazine called 5¢ *Review*. Back in Vancouver I covered the Kosmik anti-baseball league for the *Georgia Straight*, in the 1970s the most famous underground newspaper in Canada. The daily Vancouver *Province*'s sports editor was Eric Whitehead, so I wrote under the name Erich Blackhead. That's how we did things in those days, but I wrote most of my jazz reviews under my own name.

Once I got really lucky. The Canadian Broadcasting Corporation fitted me with a soundman, and we went to Santa Barbara to do a profile on Diane Jones, who was training to represent Canada in the pentathlon at the 1976 Olympics. This was in early spring. I got a sunburn along the part in my hair.

But you have to grow older in your trade, and you have to drop most of your occupations. I dropped sportswriting, photography, acting, jazz criticism, playwriting, cartooning, songwriting, badminton, and beer.

Still, when people introduce me at a panel discussion or a reading, they say poet, novelist, short-story writer, critic, and radio person. I like it that way. In the U.S., I would probably be thought a dilettante, but in Canada we cross boundaries often. People suspect us of being smugglers. Michael Ondaatje smuggled himself into his book "by" Billy the Kid, and he smuggled Billy the Kid into his book about Buddy Bolden in turn-of-the-century New Orleans.

bp Nichol said that I write essays like stories and stories like essays. I like that, too. Writing an essay, unless it is the kind of essay I used to find to my dismay in the *Kenyan Review*, can be as much fun as writing a story. Writing a poem is a duty.

QUICKNESS HAS ALWAYS BEEN my favourite quality. My father in heaven is probably thinking about how slow I was mixing concrete when we were building our house in Oliver. I dont like the quickness of our cat with the goldfinches, but I liked the quickness of Clyde the Glide Drexler going around Vlady Divac for a layup in the fourth quarter.

It usually takes me seven years to get a novel written, but when I am sitting in some foreign town writing it I like to go quickly. Quick is not the same as fast. Lots of baseball players are fast but you have to be quick to become a great base stealer. I like the prose of Jerome Charyn because though he writes pretty long novels his sentences are quick. Quick means alive rather than monumental.

Some people's novels are fast food, and that is no more interesting than a McDonald's shake.

Even with my bad back, I go along sidewalks quick. I slip between slowpokes. They might be listening to some white boys' bam bam on their Walkmans. I'm skipping by. I'm trying to walk like Charlie Parker on "Happy Bird Blues."

My pulse is fast. My hands, people have always told me, are warm. I wanted to be a drummer but I gave it up. The snare brushes I bought in Winnipeg on a winter's day in 1956 are now hanging on the fireplace in my study. Jack Kerouac ran down the Matterhorn in California, like writing (you can run like water, or like lightning. Kerouac did it like writing.) In Oliver I liked to run down a fan of shale slide. You had to take another giant step before you knew where you were going to put your foot. I used to tell people that before I read William Carlos Williams, that shale was the most important influence on my poetry.

Whenever I get into a radio station and on the air I start talking and thinking very quickly. My first book, *Points on the Grid*, didnt come out till I was twenty-eight, but the poems go quick—not very good but quick. I know I'm reading well when my voice is quick. When I'm reading someone else's book silently I am one of the slowest readers in bookland, but when I'm reading one of my books out loud I zip.

If I do a crossword—zip. If I give a lecture—zip. One night in a hotel room in Melbourne I spoke my confessional autobiography full of fiction, quick as a wink, for four hours to a bunch of sleepyheads—zip. But this piece you are reading? I've been on it for two weeks, a zip at a time.

READING IS WHAT I DO with my life. This is an answer to the schoolboys who saw me always with a book and said, "Why dont you live life instead of reading about it?" What could I do? I somehow caught on how to read before I went to grade one in Greenwood. Parents told their kids that the war would end sometime and that the Allies would win it. I greeted that idea with mixed feelings. I thought that once the war was over there would be no more newspapers.

I read while I'm eating, of course. I actually did read

under the covers with a flashlight on school nights. I read on the stationary bike at my gym; I wear industrial ear-protectors against the loud teenager music they play there. I read popular magazines while watching ball games on television. I read literary magazines between books. I'm a year behind on *Paideuma* and *Japan Quarterly*. I used to have a pile of books I had to read immediately. Then I had a big bookcase of them. When Thea got old enough, I took over her playroom across from my study, and now I have a room full of books I must read immediately. I read slowly, so if I dont add any books to the room I should finish it around A.D. 2040. But over the past couple of decades I've spent eleven dollars a day on books. I used to read three newspapers a day, but now read only one or two, unless I'm travelling.

I'm always remembering how lovely and magical reading a novel used to be, and feel sorry for myself that the gleam has gone while I've grown more knowledgeable. But I think that if I'm lucky enough to be reading in A.D. 2010, I'll look back on the Thomas Hardy novel I've just read and remember, fondly, the excitement.

On the Toronto subway and in Air Canada 767s, I notice a lot of people reading books. But it saddens me to see that almost all of them are reading thick bestsellers by some U.S. American whose name I vaguely recognize—Ken Follet, say. When I see someone reading a book of literature I want to hug her. I'd probably find out that she has to read it for a course she's taking. But one time Smaro Kamboureli paid me a great compliment: while flying to Venezuela to attend her brother's wedding, she read two books, my book of poems, *Kerrisdale Elegies*, and the latest translation of Jacques Derrida.

S CHOOL WAS ALWAYS something I liked, and perversely, admitted to liking. Work, with very few exceptions, was not. Eventually I figured it out—that the reason I liked school was that it kept me away from work.

When I left home at the age of seventeen to go to college in Victoria, it was with the comfort that it would keep me away from full-time work till spring. Spring used to depress me.

After I got my B.A. in history from the University of British Columbia, where I had gone after three years of work and goofing off in the air force, I faced a crisis. A B.A. in history did not prepare one for anything but work, or a graduate program in history. Things were going too fast. I was twenty-four years old. I registered as an "unclassified" student, neither grad nor undergrad, and took a heavy program of literature courses: Chaucer, Shakespeare, eighteenth century, Japanese literature, and the twentieth century. It was the neatest year I ever spent in school.

Then I had the opportunity to avoid a full-time job for another couple years, while pursuing an M.A. in English. A professor said that while doing so I should be a teaching assistant for two hundred dollars a month. I said no, I'd be too scared, I'll just be a marker. Teaching assistant, he said. So I taught and marked first-year English students. In my second year of grad school I also taught literature to third-year engineers and foresters, and got an additional hundred dollars a month.

While doing this, I also wrote a 550-page novel and hundreds of poems, acted in a few plays, helped edit *Tish*, wrote book reviews, put stickers on windshields in a parking lot, wrote a weekly column for the *Ubyssey*, UBC's campus paper, wrote another weekly column for the Oliver *Chronicle*, and worked on my papers and thesis. I was in school because I didnt want to have to find and keep a full-time job.

But then I graduated, and before I could figure out what they were doing to me, I had a full-time job teaching at the University of Alberta in Calgary, for $5,200 a year. A hundred times my unlucky number. Angela and I had a furnished apartment with the lawn at eye level, and I became the superintendent to cut down on the rent payments. I shovelled a lot of snow.

Later I taught at Sir George Williams University in Montreal and at Simon Fraser University in Burnaby. Teaching is not as good as writing, but it is better than working.

THEA BOWERING is a name that has begun to show up in literary magazines. Of course the author writes both poems and stories.

When Angela Luoma and I got married we were both students, and very soon I was a teacher. We made a deal that we would not have an offspring for the first five years of our marriage. This way we were able to go to Mexico in the summer, after I taught at summer school for some more money. The first time I drove the ten-year-old Chevrolet I bought from my father, and then the next year we flew down in a DC-8. We spent a lot of wonderful time with our dear friends Margaret Randall and Sérgio Mondragón, who kept having children and editing *El corno emplumado*. My second book, *The Man in Yellow Boots*, was published in Mexico.

When the five years were up, we had just moved to Montreal. I said what about having an offspring, and Angela said not this year. A year or two later she said what about a little Bowering, so we did but we didnt have an offspring that year.

During our last year in Montreal we went to New York City after Christmas, and came home on New Year's Eve. We were supposed to go to a big party across Grosvenor Avenue, but after New York City we said let's just go to bed instead. We bowered, and Thea Bowering was conceived either at the end of 1970 or the beginning of 1971.

I grew impatient with the industrial residue we found on our many windowsills every morning, so we shook the dust of Montreal. Angela and uterine Thea flew to the West Coast in a B-747, and I drove our six-year-old Chevrolet and two chihuahuas across the country, and we took up residence in a commune on York Avenue in Vancouver.

I began writing instead of teaching, and every week we drove across Burrard Inlet to our birth classes. Eventually we got together with Dr. Herstein and Nurse Davidson and a lot of other people in the delivery room at Vancouver General, and had Thea Bowering. It was, as people such as we usually say, the best night of our lives. When that head and then the rest emerged the way they were foretold in the birth classes, I uttered those characteristic early-seventies words, "Oh, wow!"

I just now heard Thea Bowering leaving the house with her lifelong best friend. They are on their way to go apartment-hunting.

*U*MBRELLAS ARE NOT for men and boys to carry, I thought, so for my first two years in Vancouver I walked around city and campus in my old air force trench coat, my hair plastered to my skull. In semi-desert Oliver it rained about five times a year, usually just in time to split the ripe cherries on the trees, for instance. If it started raining, chances were that the sun was still out in part of the sky, and in half an hour you could go out on your bicycle or picking ladder again. When I came to the Coast and it started to rain I would step into a downtown doorway to wait it out. I could have starved to death.

I saw male students holding big black umbrellas over themselves, but big-city ways are the slope to dissipation, I reasoned. In Oliver I had never seen a man carry an umbrella. I had never seen a man push a shopping cart, either.

After a couple of years of plastered hair I acquired an umbrella and an ability to be patronizing toward small semi-desert towns. Here is the way you acquired an umbrella: you went to the university lost and found; you maintained that you had misplaced an umbrella; when asked to describe it, you mentioned that it was black with a brown wooden handle. Yes, that's the one, you said.

But I still hate the rain. I live where it rains forty or fifty centimetres a year, and I still take the rain, especially on a day when I am scheduled to play ball, as a personal affront. Once on a rainy day I inquired of my ten-year-old daughter, "Dont you just detest the rain?" She replied, "No, of course not, it's just the weather."

I do not carry an umbrella any more. I have a rain hat and a semi-waterproof jacket. I am two men in one—I am the urbane man of letters who has read Roland Barthes profitably, and who is familiar with this city, perhaps with an earlier version of it. But inside that guy is the Oliver boy, a somehow more pure human being who was thrust up by a terrain that God had in mind—greasewood, sagebrush, ponderosa, cactus, sandy cutbank, quick diamondback in the garden.

I never used the word "garden" to refer to flowers until I had lived in Vancouver for at least a decade. Back home a garden is back of your house (sometimes in front, too) where the tomato leaves are prickly and fuzzy in the sun.

VANCOUVER IS MY HOME, though, and while it often crosses my mind to start living somewhere else, Toronto or Adelaide, for instance, there isnt really anywhere else that would be as good as this place. When I am in Arizona or New Mexico, I have an odd feeling that that's where I was meant to spend my life. It must be the climate speaking to my subconscious, if I have one. But though I like to walk around in a T-shirt in Tucson, I do not like guns and jet fighter planes and atom bombs.

Visitors and the local public relations people often remark on Vancouver's natural beauty. But the longer people have lived here, the less natural beauty there is. Real estate monsters litter subdivisions higher up the mountains, and where the trees used to be, the rain-beaten earth slides downhill. In 1960, my girlfriend and I ran a boat to Passage

Island and found the beach covered with condoms. I wondered how many sexually agitated people could have made
it to that generally empty spot. She instructed me regarding
toilets and sewers and ocean tides.

But if you like the margins of culture, while not desiring
to flee it altogether, Vancouver is a good place to write. The
novelists who most often make the covers of magazines,
Margaret Atwood, Timothy Findley, Michael Ondaatje,
and Alice Munro, live in Toronto or a quick ride from that
city. The most highly touted up-and-comers have arrived in
Toronto from other places in the British Commonwealth
of Nations.

Toronto is the centre of the country, and while it is no
Paris, people who write with eyes for a career head there
from the provinces. Vancouver tends to be a place for losers
or people who cannot fit in or artists who want to protect
their marginality. If you want a career in the magazines, you
have to put up with snow and hard-winter wind off Lake
Ontario and sickening humidity in the summer.

Torontonians envy and pity Vancouverites for their easier life and underdeveloped ambition. They say, my, what a
gorgeous little baseball stadium, and phew, how can you
understand the poetry in that magazine?

So I continue to live in Vancouver, a kind of exile ame-
liorated by Air Canada and the Canadian Broadcasting
Corporation. When I lived back east I got phoned a lot for
"assignments." Here I find the time to write, and play ball
in February.

WRITING IS INTERESTING. I mean the act, I guess
it is, of writing. The fun we call the work, ever
since André Gide called it that. Part of it is deciding how to write the novel or the serial poem, or say, this
alphabiography. This is being written by pen (Pilot Precise
V5), double-spaced in a series of university examination

booklets with the covers torn off. I dont think that makes it academic writing, does it?

My father had a beaten old black portable typewriter with round keys, so I wrote my Oliver *Chronicle* baseball and basketball reports on that, typing with my middle fingers because my father did it that way, his right forefinger having been lost to a timber saw before I knew him.

A lot of corny movies about novelists, and the poetics learned from Charles Olson, persuaded one to compose on the typewriter, even poems, except those you wrote on the inside back covers of paperbacks at the Varsity Cafe. But in 1970 in an Irish section of London, England, I began to write a book that would be called *Autobiology*, and for a decade I wrote just about everything by hand, to slow me down. I just had to choose the paper to write on, sometimes a nifty sketchbook a friend brought back from Japan, or school scribblers (a lot of writers use those, I have found out), depending on the size of the "work."

For the novel *Burning Water*, I went to Chinatown and bought a number of thick hardcover notebooks made in the People's Republic and called "Sailing Ship." Robin Blaser had showed me one at his house. They were perfect because ten pages held a thousand words, a Trieste day's writing about George Vancouver's sailing ships. I decided to stay home and write my next two novels, the second of which was *Caprice*, directly into the word processor, my first computer, an Apple II expanded to 64K. People always asked whether it made a difference to the novel.

And so on. For a few years I was writing journalism and radio stuff on the computer, letters on my IBM Selectric typewriter, and poetry and essays by hand. While I was writing this piece by hand, I was also collaborating with Angela in a sequence of meditations on pictures. I was writing directly into my Macintosh Classic, and she was writing by hand on a pad of foolscap. We were also collaborating with

Mike Matthews and David Bromige on a nostalgic novel. That was being done with a Mac Classic, an IBM PC, a NEC, a Mac SE, and three copying machines. Now that was fun.

EROGRAPHY ARRIVED during my writing lifetime, thank goodness. It made it possible for us to compose collaborative novels through the mail, of course. Marginalized poets could make local magazines if they knew someone who worked in an office with lax security. Writers who wanted to create text with a visual organization or disorganization could design manuscripts to challenge any publisher. But then unscrupulous schoolteachers could pirate our poems for the classes in contemporary relevancy.

We all know Luddite writers who refuse even to teach themselves to type, who lock themselves into garrets, there to fashion sonnets or family chronicles with ostrich-plume pens by candlelight. But others among us cheer for every new magic machine that comes along to make text production less a drudge. I am known to be too shy to buy a new shirt, but I like buying gizmos when I get big enough chunks of sudden money. I've bought seven personal computers and we still have five of them in the house (or in the car).

My old *Tish* friends, Frank Davey, Fred Wah, and Lionel Kearns, got their first computers as soon as such things became available, and I followed shortly. In the early 1980s, they began a lovely experiment, something called *Swift Current*. Continuing our interest in innovative magazine creation, it was an electronic literary forum, a magazine fed by writers with modems. Subscribers could pick and choose from the menu, invent their own table of contents. Readers could print out their favourite material. It was a very democratic way of assembling a journal—especially if you were well off enough to get access to a modem. There were not many single mothers among the contributors.

Still, it was quite different from a glossy quarterly offering learned articles and new poems received at the editor's address a year or two earlier, written a year before that. In *Swift Current* you could read the review of a book before the book was between covers.

Xerography is probably the widest purveyor of literature, though. It can save time and effort and occluded texts. One week Angela used my home copier to capture Sheila Watson's 555-page 1965 dissertation on Wyndham Lewis. That dissertation is usually buried in the University of Toronto library. It is longer than all Watson's fiction books put together, and nearly as heavy as was the author herself. But she will never be duplicated.

*Y*OUTH, JUST AS THEY have always told us, does slip away. Writers, though, can keep on writing about their youth, even as their bodies fall apart around them. They can feed off it. While other people regret, they can exploit. What a peculiar Cartesian experience—look at Jack Kerouac, getting fat and big-nose and boozy while he wrote about Ti-Jean running beautiful down another track or football field. Samuel Beckett was notoriously bedevilled by Descartes. So all his "characters" are decrepit men and women, old as a soothsayer in a jug, even while Beckett was hopping down a Paris street.

Still, though it can be their bread and butter, writers I know miss their youth more than regular people do. I think it may be that being a mature author with a back-cover photograph proving one's august immovability from the literary scene has not proven to be as enjoyable as being a very little known poet or fiction writer with the ignited hope of dazzling people.

I cannot remember when journalists and editors stopped referring to me as one of my country's most promising new writers, and then one of my country's most accomplished young writers. I do recall that such nonsense went on longer than I thought it should. Now they always introduce me as a person who has won two Governor General's Awards, written an enormous number of books, and become some kind of semi-illustrious gent. The part of me that is interested in my youth hates to hear that.

When I was fifteen, working in the orchard near Naramata, I stepped backward off my ladder with seventy pounds of apples in the picking bag strapped to my chest. I had forgotten that this part of the orchard was sloped toward the clay cliff overlooking Lake Okanagan. I stepped back farther than I expected to and cracked a lumbar vertebra. I had a sore back when I stood at attention in the air force honour guard, and now I have a sore back because I play second base. For forty years I have had a sore back every minute. Sometimes it gets worse, even ambulance worse. Sometimes it makes me walk like those old guys we have all seen walking past the bus station.

It's a legacy from my youth.

It goes away for a while when I am fast asleep. I have always refused to sleep in the daytime, because I hate to have hours of my life happen when I dont know about it.

But everyone has to sleep sometime....

 Z Z Z Z Z Z

GROWING A WRITER

More Pencils, More Books

T HE THREE-AND-A-HALF-FOOT person walks in brand new brown oxfords to the school bus door, carrying a brand new Jetsons (Star Wars, Barbie, Smurfs, Big Bird, Barney, Teletubbies) lunch kit filled with more food than she is likely to eat in a week. Behind her, in the doorway of the house, stands the mother, tidy hair and clean apron, a wave of the hand, and natural eyelashes beating back tears.

How often have you seen that picture? Yes, and you know what's going through the larger person's head: there she goes already, into a new world of companionship and stimuli, and here stand I, after these few quick years, suddenly lonely.

Chances are, though, she doesnt have much time to pine, because she has to get her stuff together to get to her own job. She doesnt remember her own first day of school, and neither do you, and neither do I. We remember, or we remember remembering, the clear and single events, the long-held and examined objects. The little girl will remember her lunch kit (though she will soon learn that paper bags are more hip), as I remember my grade-one handkerchiefs. They were small and patterned all over with English bulldogs protecting the Empire.

But the first day of school is a mess and a movement, a dislocation to be sure. It leaves no impression, because the reason for schooling has begun. The reason that kid is sent out of the house and into that other building, that bigger building, that building where nothing belongs to anyone, where you use things they have there but you cant take them home. The reason is that, frankly, the kid has to be socialized. She has to become a component in the machine that sends bills and newspapers to her parents' house.

So much for companionship. My first schoolroom was grade one, two, and three, grade threes closest to the windows, in the downstairs north room of the school at the bottom of the mountain in Greenwood, B.C., during World War II, and I sat there wondering how long this holding a pencil and getting ready to fight the Gerries would last.

When you're five and a half years old and you move out of your mother's familiar fiefdom with the kittens behind the kitchen stove, into the massive machine of even a four-room school, your mother and even your teacher, too young to be your mother, might see you as a happy shrieking child running around the playground dust with your playmates. But that's not what you see, and that's not what I saw.

I mean I didnt *know* any of these people, and lots of them looked dangerous. In fact, some of them were, the ones who rolled boulders down off the mountain into the playground, trying to hit the love-hate building, or the kid who jumped off the teeter-totter when his end was down, and dropped me on my elbow on the rocks. I wore a sling for two weeks. Or the grade-four tykes who at last succeeded in burning down the Greenwood school a few months after we had moved, thank the Lord, away from town.

What I mean is: when I moved to school I began feeling for the first time what I have always felt since—that I was alone, that somehow that was always waiting for me, there.

It wasnt till grade eight that I admitted out loud that I liked school, and I may have done so from the start. But that had nothing to do with the people there. It had to do with *me* there.

I was, earlier, I have to admit, a dropout from kindergarten. I dont know how long I spent there, maybe a week. But I remember that I thought it was a pretty strange place. I see an orange-coloured paper chain, and I remember taking one look and deciding, rightly, that I could never make such a thing. I somehow managed to get out and go back to the big something tree in the back lane, a garter snake in my pocket, and to hang out with the comics from the *Star Weekly* that came to us via the drugstore every Tuesday from what seemed to be the real Canada. In the winter there was lots of room on the hill for my Radio sleigh, the kind you have to steer with your feet in the snow.

Alone.

I was lucky. I didnt learn to talk till I was three, but I learned to read when I was four going on five. I have a sad memory of one of my first books: a young Donald Duck is late for school, or he refuses to go in, he's sitting on the steps, listening to the teacher and children inside chanting, "Take away six, drop the five, carry the three," and so on, and he is trying to imagine what they're moving around in there. I pictured this happening on the back fire-escape steps of the school in Greenwood, B.C., and guess who was Donald Duck? I was already then sad and wise, and five and a half years old. Outside it all, but filling up my Jolly Numbers exercise book by the third week of September.

You want to know how much a grade-one kid is alone? The worst thing that can happen to you is that you wet your pants. No, come to think of it, that's the second worst. The worst happened to me, too.

But the worst permutation of that second-worst thing is that you wet your pants and you're sitting there trying to be invisible, and the cheery, caring young teacher gets you to stand up and recite some canonical words in front of the class, and you're not, though you hoped hard, dry yet. More socialization.

You do it, and then you run for the door instead of your desk; and she lets you, and the fact that she lets you does not go unnoticed. It means that it is serious enough, and she agrees that you have done something awful and unwelcome in this conventionalized new world.

You want to know how really, really isolated I was? On

the way to school next morning, filled with dread at having to return for eleven and a half more years, I noted in the lane a small, yes, crotch-sized puddle, and invented my desperate story of how I happened to fall in just such a way that....

I'll tell you, I cant remember the name or the face of any of my classmates, or my teachers, in that school in Greenwood, B.C. But I can remember some things. The huge brown paper sheets with little holes in them—you held them up to the blackboard and banged on the holes with blackboard brushes full of coloured chalk dust, and made outline pictures of elephants and daisies and South America. The green stuff someone sprinkled on the oily wooden floor of the classroom sometime during the weekend. The war-saving stamps, blue or pink or brown, with pictures of tanks and airplanes and WACS on them. Someone at school took your dime and you licked the stamps and stuck them in your book, and so did your sister, and in seven years you were supposed to get five dollars for every four you spent. Across the line, you heard, the Yankee kids just had to spend three dollars to get four. That's another thing I learned in school today, Mum.

Now World War II is over. Teachers usually dont have to handle three grades in one room. Schools have hot lunch cafeterias and milk programs, and a nearby McDonald's. They have smart teachers who take Psychology in the Department of Education. But still your daughter, even if you do drive her to school in your station wagon, is going to go into a big place painted in primary colours, and at home they dont have words on the doors.

Think about how lonely you are looking for wilted leaves on the lettuce at the IGA. But dont imagine for a minute that your kid is sitting on the top rung of the monkey bars with all her classmates, saying, "We're all going to be real estate professionals."

And dont ask her what she learned in school today. You know you've tried it before, and she just shuffled her feet in her scuffed brown oxfords and said, "I can't remember." She knows by your question that you, too, are part of the conspiracy to get her where she's going.

That's what I told myself, anyway, a while back. Yesterday I saw my daughter writing a short story on her old Mac. I was bringing her mail. She had an envelope from Revenue Canada.

Deking Dad

IS IT JUST ME, OR HAVE you noticed this, too? It seems as if every time successful writers or artists write magazine pieces or undergo interviews or give conference talks full of advice for young writers or artists, they like to recall being antisocial troublemakers when they were kids. Somehow being an antisocial troublemaker is a good sign that you are going to grow up to be a successful writer or artist.

My old friend the successful writer Susan Musgrave confessed to a misspent youth in an article in *In 2 Print*, the young people's magazine from Port Colborne. In high school she necked with her boyfriend in biology class, forged notes from her parents, and dropped some mind-expanding drugs on the beach. Heck, I knew someone who did all those things, too, except that the necking took place in math class. This guy is now washing windshields in the Esso station in my home town.

My mother still lives in my home town. It's called Oliver, B.C., on the government maps, and Lawrence in my short stories. My mother often tells people that when I was a high school kid I made her life miserable with my antisocial behaviour. I dont remember it that way at all. I always thought of myself as a secret lonely hero of virtue. Okay, I did get expelled from school a few times. In grade ten I got expelled for walking to the water fountain when they played "God Save the King," and for sticking anti-King notes in the library books. I figured this was an example of virtue: I was sticking up for a free Canada. In grade eleven I got expelled for organizing a bunch of classmates to refuse to buy another textbook halfway through the school year. I forget what I got expelled for in grade twelve. They let me into the school to write my final exams, and then out I went.

I wasnt a juvenile delinquent. In fact, I once had the ambition to be a policeman, to fight crime the way my hero Batman did, to make the world safe for virtue. This ambition came to an end one day in Penticton, B.C., when I saw the peculiar way the policemen there got a native man out of a restaurant and into a police car. At that moment I thought: someone ought to be writing about this. But meanwhile I was nearly always in trouble at school. I just could not keep quiet when I thought of a funny remark. I may not have been a juvenile delinquent, but I was the class clown. I could often be found standing in the hall outside a classroom I had been ejected from, or hauling rocks from the schoolyard to the rockpile. This was back when you could get punished at school. I got the strap three times, twice on the hands, once elsewhere.

The situation was a little tough on my family. My father was the chemistry teacher at that high school. He was sort of my hero.

I mean Oliver, B.C., was a dinky little place surrounded by orchards in the Okanagan Valley. My father was the only person I ever saw writing something. He wrote stuff on an old square black portable typewriter that he never even took out of the case, just plunked it on his little desk and opened the lid. I loved that typewriter. My father typed with his two middle fingers because he had cut his right forefinger off with a timber saw. For about twenty years I typed with my middle fingers, too. I also shot a .22 rifle at air cadets with my right middle finger, having watched my father. My father was kind of my wounded hero. When he was umpiring baseball games it often looked as if he was indicating one and a half strikes.

Here's what he typed with those two middle fingers, while he hummed some corny old dad song: sports. He was the baseball and basketball reporter for the Oliver *Chronicle* and the Penticton *Herald*. Once I learned how to make that typewriter work, I never thought of being a policeman or anything else that involved moving people from one place to another. I wanted to be a sportswriter. Forget lonely virtue, I decided, how can I ease my father out of this sports-writing job?

I ought to mention that I copied him in various other ways, too. He was always reading when he wasnt teaching school or picking apples or playing cards with my mother. The daily newspaper, the *Star Weekly*, including its prepublication "novels," Erle Stanley Gardner mysteries, baseball magazines, teachers' magazines, novels about surgeons in the U.S. Civil War, and so on. I asked him about the weekly comics, and he said he read them all except "Jane Arden," so I quit reading "Jane Arden." Every week there was a cut-out dress with tabs that your sister could put on her cardboard Jane. It was also from my father that I learned that you should carry something to read in case you got stuck in a lineup at the post office.

I managed to deke him out of his sportswriting jobs, though. It started with reading. My parents got me a subscription to *Sport* magazine for Christmas. I still have every copy that ever came in the mail. Pretty soon I was spending all my change on baseball and hockey magazines. I would read every article from beginning to end, and I would read every inch of the sports pages in the Vancouver *Sun*, and pretty soon I knew how to be a sportswriter. First I wrote up some of my own versions of the ball games the Oliver teams were playing. Then I started sitting with my father while he was doing his business as "official scorekeeper." That sounded really good. At the high school basketball games in the winter we sat at a courtside table, along with the time-keeper, across from the bleachers. But baseball had its own excitement: we climbed up through a trap door onto the roof of the shaky old wooden grandstand, and crept right up to the front, to a little boarded-in room with a chicken-wire front, right over home plate. Sometimes my father let me keep score, and sometimes I filled in on the public address while the regular guy was away getting soft ice cream.

By the time I was sixteen, I was the official scorer and the reporter for the *Chronicle* and the *Herald*. From the *Chronicle* I got fifteen cents an inch for my stories, but from the *Herald* I was pulling in twenty-five cents an inch. My father showed me how to cut out the stories and measure them and send them in for my cheque every month.

I wasnt antisocial. I was a sportswriter. I was doing something no one else I knew was doing. I was the only sportswriter in town. Cool, I thought, because that was the word we used way back then.

So I was going to be a sportswriter. I even carried my editor's camera and made my own pictures for the paper. My buddy Will and I had a darkroom in his basement. We were the only photographer kids in town.

But I was reading a lot of different things, and sports wasnt the only thing I was writing. I read just about every western novel published in the twentieth century. I read science fiction and sports novels. The first poetry book I ever bought by myself was written by a sportswriter. I still have a copy. Okay, I could be a sportswriter *and* a poet. I would be the only poet in town. As it turned out I was the only poet in the Okanagan Valley, until Pat Lane showed up, a guy with a cigarette in his mouth, a pool cue in one hand, and a pen in the other. Now *there* was a juvenile delinquent. But he was from the North Okanagan. Now he is a very successful poet.

There was a weekly newspaper put out by students in my school. It was called *The Scroll*. I didnt have anything to do with it, because I was a professional reporter. But I did work on the school annual. And I did publish poems in the school annual. One of my favourites was forty stanzas long, all about headhunters in Malacca. To this day I dont know whether there were any headhunters in that part of the world. In those days there werent any creative writing teachers in high school advising you to write about what you know. Thank goodness. If you write about what you know, you will keep on writing the same thing, and you will never know any more than you do now.

Whenever writer kids ask me what to write about I always tell them: try writing about something you dont know. And while you are at it, I say, forget that creative writing advice about using your own voice. Listen for some strange voice, I tell them. Look at the successful poet David McFadden, I tell them. He is always writing stuff he doesnt know anything about, and he is always swiping someone else's voice to write it in. He's really good, just like Susan Musgrave and Pat Lane. When he was a kid in Hamilton, Ontario, he was usually doing something no one else in town was doing, as far as he knew.

I'll tell you something I used to do when I was twelve, as an example. In those days Nabisco Shredded Wheat used to come in that box of twelve with grey rectangles of cardboard between the layers of biscuits. Three cardboards to a box. We ate a lot of Shredded Wheat in our family.

I found out that the letter-writing paper my parents used was just the right size to cover one side of one of those grey cardboard things, with enough overlap to glue the edges on the back. It was nice paper. It was called "linen." I used it to start my famous comic-strip characters collection. The comic strips in those days were quite a lot like the movies. An earlier invention of mine was the shoebox theatre: I would get a few months' worth of some comic strip such as "Steve Canyon," and glue them end to end, and make a reel to crank through a slot at one end of a shoebox. There would be a skylight right over the strip and a peephole at the other end of the shoebox. Most of the movies I saw when I was in grade three were showing in my shoebox theatre.

Anyway, I was saying that the comic strips were like the movies. For instance, some of the panels would have close-ups of the characters. I decided that I would put five close-ups on each of my famous characters cards. I used the window to trace with pencil and eventually used my father's India ink to finish off the job. So one of my cards might have pictures of Steve Canyon, Little Lulu, Donald Duck, Dagwood, and Wonder Woman.

They were beautiful. I made about forty of them. I dont have a clue where they went. I also dont know where my homemade Big League Baseball game records and statistics went. I dont know why exactly, but when I make poems or stories now I feel a lot like the way I felt when I was making those comic-strip cards, and I was the only person in town making them. I have found out that other writers used to make peculiar things when they were kids. David McFadden and I are big fans of Jack Kerouac, the French-Canadian writer who happened to be born and raised in the United States, and when Jack Kerouac was a kid he made all kinds of things—baseball leagues, adventure magazines, theatrical plays. He was the only kid in Lowell, Massachusetts, making these things.

Jack and David and I were nerds, I guess. Nowadays we think of nerd kids as computer freaks, making weird games and other programs. But they are not the only kids in town doing it. The real McCoy might be that strange young person down in the family basement making a relief map of Canada out of dry pasta. If I had to bet on who would turn out to be a successful writer, the pasta kid or all those people making a big noise at the 7-Eleven parking lot, I would bet on the pasta kid.

Poems for Men

THE FIRST BOOK OF POETRY I ever read was volume ten of a set of books my parents had. There were volumes on geography and wildlife and astronomy and so on. Each volume was a separate colour, and volume ten was pink. I read all the books, but it was volume ten that got beaten up with use. When I think back on my childhood I am kind of surprised by that. I didnt actually buy a book of poetry till I was fifteen.

I didnt have much money to buy stuff, but I bought comic books, mainly *Detective Comics* and *Batman* and *World's Finest*. These three all had the Caped Crusader in them. My mother made me get rid of them. I never let her forget how much a *World's Finest* number one would sell for now. When I was eleven I decided that it was time to start buying movie magazines. I didnt know that boys didnt buy movie magazines. I went down to Frank's and bought *Screen Gems* and *Photoplay* for a year, reading about Lana Turner, and gazing at still photos of movies I would never see.

When I was twelve I went down to Frank's and bought sports magazines, starting with *Sport*. The first one I ever bought had Frank Brimsek on the cover, and it would be a long time till they had another hockey player there. I bought *Sport Life* and *Baseball Digest* and all the rest. It was a hobby I kept up till I was about twenty-three. I still have piles of those magazines, and I am starting to look for someone to sell them to.

When I was fifteen I went to Frank's and bought my first book of poems. Frank's was one of the two poolrooms in Oliver. The other one had a cafe in front. Frank's was a poolroom with a one-chair barber and a tobacco stand up front. It had an old dark wooden floor. Frank did not specialize in poetry books. He sold mainly twenty-five-cent westerns, many of which I spent my pin-setting money on.

But when I was fifteen I bought *Poems for Men* by Damon Runyan. It was published by Permabooks of Garden City, New York. Permabooks were thirty-five cents each, and when they started they had those stiff covers you would find on children's picture books, though *Poems for Men* has a normal poolroom paperback cover.

Until I was twenty-two I always gave books away after I had read them. But when I was twenty-six I found a used copy of *Poems for Men*, and I have kept this one. People always hint that they would like to have it, but all they get is permission to read a poem or two.

Of course I knew Damon Runyan from the sports magazines. Next to Grantland Rice, he was my favourite sportswriter, and I wanted to be a sportswriter. I had read a lot of Runyan's short stories. My whole idea of New York City came from the settings and characters of Damon Runyan. Still do. Last year I flew to Phoenix to see a spring training baseball game. That night I stayed in my hotel and watched the movie *Guys and Dolls* on television.

Damon Runyan joined the army when he was fourteen, and went to the Philippines to join the U.S. American war against Spain. A lot of his poems are about ordinary soldiers:

> Scenery there was plenty, sir, the like I never
>   have seen:
> Some of it struck me as brownish-like, and
>   some of it mighty green.
> Some of the roads were muddy, sir, and some
>   of them pretty fine,
> As I hiked up with Dickman—old Joe
>   Dickman—to the Rhine!

Now I am kind of hoping that in terms of form and diction I was never influenced by Damon Runyan. I never looked for a girlfriend like Lana Turner, either. But I respect Damon Runyan and the world he invented. I have never been able to decide whether his ballads are naive or cynical. I would find enough of the cynical in the book of poems I bought at Frank's when I was seventeen, *New Poems by American Poets*, edited by Rolfe Humphries and published at thirty-five cents by Ballantine Books of New York.

Poems for Men are about pool shooters and racehorse bettors and boxing pugs and dice-throwers, as everyone would expect of Damon Runyan. But I first knew Runyan as a baseball writer, and I am pretty sure that though I would be led into all of his New York and other worlds, I first checked out his baseball poems. Say, have you ever heard "Opening Day"?

> There's a bang in the whang
> Of the first-round clang
> For a battle of fistic cracks.
> There's a kick in the click
> Of a barrier's flick
> As the horses tear up the tracks.
> There's a thrill in the trill
> Of the whistle shrill
> That starts the football play.
> But, say—
> Give me the thrill
> In the springtime chill
> Of baseball's opening day!

Now you are thinking of the title. I often have, ever since I first saw it. I guess that in 1951, poetry, like opera and flower shows, was mainly for women, eh? Keats and Dickinson—you can understand that. But men didnt have to shy away from the idea totally, not as long as there was a "Cremation of Sam McGee," or Damon Runyan's card sharps and racetrack touts, inhabiting ballads that bounced between witticism and pathos.

My Heart in Hiding

HEN I WAS IN HIGH SCHOOL my favourite serious poets were Dylan Thomas and Hart Crane. Young people ought to read Dylan Thomas and let him swarm all over them. In later years they will probably think that they have outgrown him. As for Hart Crane—when I was a high school kid I had no idea how difficult Crane was. But I was fascinated by what he did on the page with the faltering airplane section of *The Bridge*.

There have been a lot of poems that turned out to be important gates in the pathway of my life, and all of them offered better metaphors than the one you have just read. After three years in the air force, I went to the University of British Columbia, and decided to read all the poetry in the PS section of the library. "PS" stands for U.S. literature. I was reading alphabetically, because I could not think of a better way to find what I was looking for. It took a while to get to *W*, of course, but eventually I found a quite newly published book called *The Desert Music* by William Carlos Williams. The title poem was so hot that the book dropped from my hands and made a loud splat on the concrete floor. From then on William Carlos Williams would be my poetry Dad.

Even while I was a UBC student, my friends and I made some kind of fuss across the country with our poetry newsletter *Tish*, and our championing of the new U.S. American poets that were unknown to our professors. They provided poems that would always stay with me and my poetry buddies, poems such as Robert Duncan's "Poem Beginning with a Line from Pindar," and Charles Olson's "Songs of Maximus" and Robert Creeley's "The Door."

These poets, who would later be called "postmodern," sprang from various traditions, including a certain U.S.

tradition of Modernists, mainly Williams and Ezra Pound. For me and my buddies, hardly a day went by when we would not read or talk about Pound's translation of Cavalcanti's "Donna mi priegha." I was particularly taken with the early Imagist poems of H.D., and later I would fall upon her wartime *Trilogy* and find the great long poem of my life. I was very proud that it had been printed originally by the Bowering Press of Plymouth.

So we were very hip young poets, the newest avant-garde, rising out of the ocean's edge to frighten the poetry old folks of Eastern Canada.

But we learned things in our actual classrooms from time to time. It was in one of those classrooms that we came upon a poem that soon we would all go around reciting. Would it surprise you to know that the poem is a sonnet? More than that, it is a Christian sonnet. More than that, it is a nineteenth-century Christian sonnet written by an Englishman!

I am talking about Gerard Manley Hopkins's "The Windhover."

Our attraction to this poem was normal, I guess. Hopkins was so avant-garde that the poem was not published till 1918, twenty-nine years after the poet's death. His poems are extravagantly vocal, and just jammed with images. Here we were, a bunch of young university poets desperate to be anti-academic; and for us, followers of Olson and Duncan and Allen Ginsberg, this meant the poem as *spoken*, and the poem as images. We were also into theorizing about poetics and composition (for which we would always be derided by the "natural" poets back east), and Gerard Manley Hopkins wrote some of the greatest compositional theory of all time. It was there in our beloved Penguin paperback of Hopkins's poems. You could look it up.

Hopkins wrote Christian sonnets because he was a monk, and thus willing to serve discipline and order. But he was an ecstatic, and needed to discover ways to burst into praise for earthly beauty. The normal tight discursive Miltonic sonnet could not hold his heart and his breath, so he found ways to stretch the lines and make the metre soar. Like a bird, maybe. Like a beautiful rebel. Sure, he was a monk, and monks are supposed to be humble and colourless. But what if your subject was God's grandeur or pied beauty? Dazzling and delicious nature are signs of God's care, and a puny poetics would never do it justice.

This is the way a Robert Frost sonnet starts:

I have been one acquainted with the night.
I have walked out in rain—and back in rain.

Already the reader knows better than to expect any soaring. It's going to be all measured walking, probably with a period at the end of the line.

Compare the first two lines of the Hopkins poem "The Windhover".

I caught this morning morning's minion, king-
  dom of daylight's dauphin, dapple-dawn-drawn
    Falcon, in his riding

It makes the Frost poem sound like prose written by a sleepy person. Imagine the nerve—to say "morning" twice in a row, to have three *m*-words followed by six *d*-words, to have twenty-six syllables (and a bit) where you are supposed to have twenty. God, we used to have fun trying to recite these lines, trying to remember "daylight's dauphin, dapple-dawn-drawn."

You couldnt help getting it a little wrong from time to time. When the young poet David Dawson and I saw each other on campus, we would wave and shout, "Hi there in your riding!"

You would never get away with something like that in an English class, but I still think it was part of learning to like and respect a great poem.

One of the things about reading Gerard Manley Hopkins was that you had to look up a lot of words, either because they were old-fashioned or because you werent old enough to have them in your vocabulary yet. So you would find out that "wimple" is that accordionated white fringe on the front of a nun's headgear. Or that "sillion" is a furrow in the farm earth. Or that "buckle" means fold up but also refers to the use of the short sword that a knight holds in his left hand while he's swinging away with his regular sword in his right hand.

That's another enjoyable thing about Hopkins's poetry, that while the sound is very lush, the poem is also packed to the bursting point with images. In these fourteen (well, fourteen plus) lines, Jesus is a windhover, all right, a hawk in the breeze, but he is also a knight, a chevalier, so there's horse stuff. The "dauphin" rimes with "Falcon," but the Dauphin is the French king's knightly son, just as Jesus is God's son. You could find out why the French called this prince the Dauphin, et cetera. Hopkins, of course, knew. But there is also ice-skating, soil-plowing, and eventually the Easter passion of Jesus. There are a million things. I will just show you a bit about the Easter stuff, as it appears in the last line.

The words that tip you off? They rime, to start with, and that is what rime is for, to make connections that will work in other ways than just sound. The words here are "fall" and "gall" and "gash." They tell of the sequence of Jesus's sacrifice, his falling while he carried his cross to the hill, the vinegar that was given to him when he asked for water, and the hole made in his side by a Roman's spear. But at the same time these words are descriptive of the burnt firewood (I have always imagined a fireplace) that all at once falls and breaks open to reveal the bright burning inside.

That's the direction Hopkins has been heading all through the poem. The windhover, he says, is masterful when it rides the wind. He says that it is in "ecstasy," which means escaping stasis. But it is more beautiful when it folds its wings and dives, presumably after its prey. Hopkins was a Jesuit, and the Jesuits liked the idea of Jesus pursuing human beings rather than just asking them to follow him. He is usually pictured as a warrior knight complete with horse and sword and buckler. Just so, the dogged working of a plow turns the earth and makes it shine.

The story of Jesus is the story of a heavenly Son who falls to earth voluntarily, all the way to earth and inside it. Hopkins says that there is the real beauty in his religion.

That is a bare outline of Hopkins's poem, maybe a hundredth of the details and ambiguities that make it, really, one of the longest poems in the English language. Any reader is welcome and encouraged to ask lots of questions. What is it about the scraping a skate's heel does as the skater makes a tight turn? Why is the poet's heart in hiding: is he a rabbit waiting for those talons? Arent there a lot of sharp things in this poem—talons, skates, spears, swords, plows? Gold-vermilion: those are the traditional colours of British kings, arent they?

Why does Hopkins use only two end-sounds in the first eight lines and only two more in the last six lines? And why does he use a one-syllable sound and a two-syllable sound in either case? Hmm, I said when I was about twenty. Hmm, I still say, even now when I know what "sillion" means, and remember that both falcons and knights wear plumes—and that poets write with them.

See, what I am saying is that such a poem is so much fun, partly because it is so lovely sounding, and partly because it compresses so many images and implications. It is the kind of poem that will last you all your life. Another good example is Shelley's "Ode to the West Wind," maybe the simplest-sounding, most complicated poem in the English language.

There are some poems that you like all your life for their startling simplicity and clarity. William Carlos Williams wrote a lot of those. But I will tell you something about a poem like "The Windhover." Decades and decades after you read it for the first time, you can sit down somewhere and open the book and read that poem, and all at once get one of those "Aha!" experiences that the best poems save up for you all through the years.

Hey, did you notice that Hopkins specified "shéer plód"? Those two downbeats sound a lot like stomping, dont they? The phrase also rimes with the line "Generations have trod, have trod, have trod" from another sonnet, "God's Grandeur." Hopkins was always doing that, too.

I am not going to perform a critical reading of "The Windhover," as they say. I would not be satisfied that I had made a start until I had burned up fifty pages. But I would like to say this: I am really glad that three decades after his death, Hopkins's poems were published by some people who did not want them to be kept from the world any longer. Thank you, as I often find myself saying to editors and other monks.

How I Wrote One of My Poems

RECENTLY I WAS LOOKING through my diary as I seldom do, and fell upon early October of 1962. U.S. president Kennedy would be starting the Cuban missile crisis in three weeks. The Berlin Wall had been up for a year. Here's what I saw in my diary for early October 1962: the handwriting of my oldest friend, Will Trump, who was my roommate at that time. Riffling a few pages, I came upon some awkward lettering done by my left hand.

Early in the morning of September 30, 1962, I broke my right hand. I did this by punching a concrete wall as hard as I could. The concrete wall had burlap pasted to it. I thought the wall was made of plaster. In recent times I had taken to punching plaster walls as an expression of my frustration with the changeable affection of my beautiful girlfriend, Angela Luoma. I was taking some chance, I thought, that my fist would strike a plaster wall just where there was a two-by-four stud, rather than dramatically crashing through plaster. So far I hadnt hit a stud—or a girlfriend, ever.

The concrete wall was in the staircase of the hipster apartment of poet Jamie Reid and filmmaker Sam Perry, overlooking the train tracks along the side of Coal Harbour. In the summer of 1963, Red Lane would do a poetry reading while standing on top of someone's Pontiac in the overgrown yard back of this apartment. Sometimes we would Frisbee Jamie's Thelonius Monk records from the balcony, trying to reach the salt water past the CPR tracks.

The reason that I punched the wall was, I think, Angela Luoma's suggestion that we let our relationship go. For a young man the worst thing to see is a loved one with someone else, and that starts with a loved one's breaking a relationship. It makes you want to hit a wall. We had been together, more or less, for a year. I had been punching walls for a month or so.

But this concrete punch seemed to do the job. Angela Luoma and I wound up sleeping together at my rickety second-storey place overlooking False Creek. I had to keep my hand on the pillow above her head. In the morning my hand had grown to be about the size of her head. We went to see the doctor, and the doctor said that the swelling had to come down before they could put a cast on. On October 2 I fell while climbing through a window for some reason, and this time my hand wasted no time in getting a message to me. I told myself that I had to get out of the youthful habit of climbing through windows. We went down to St. Paul's Hospital on Burrard Street, and Angela Luoma sat on a bus stop bench across from the hospital while the doctors and nurses put me into a daze and fixed my hand. I remember a needle going in between bones. I remember waking up in an empty operating room with faint light coming from concave lamps.

On October 5 they put a plaster cast on my hand and wrist and forearm, and I hated it. It was as hard as concrete. It held some of my fingers straight and some of them crooked. I went around sniffing at it—the odour was really something, irresistible. When you have a heavy cast on your hand you are always banging it into door frames and furniture. I was a teaching assistant at UBC. Eighteen-year-olds helped me gather my notes after class.

It was a bad time to be one-handed. I had bought a $400 Austin, my third and most expensive car, and entered a raffle at the car dealer's. On the night of the draw, Angela Luoma and I were sitting in Scott's Cafe on Granville Street. Abruptly, I rose and tried to get my jacket over my shoulder.

"What?" she asked, looking ruefully at her full cup of java.

"Wait here," I said. "I have to go over to Burrard Street. They're going to pull my name out of a barrel."

At the car dealer's there was some cheesy radio jocko and some car salesmen in blazers. Behind them was a tree that had one-dollar bills all over it instead of leaves. There were a few two-dollar bills, too. As a guy in a blazer and a marsh-mallow grin reached down into the barrel, I was already trying to get my jacket off my unbroken arm. The guy looked at the piece of paper in his hand as if it were a poem by Margaret Avison.

"G. Bo Ring," he said.

"That is I," I said, in a white shirt.

I had one minute to pick money off a tree and put it into a basket. Bad news: I could use only my left hand. Good news: I am from the Okanagan Valley. I picked fruit for a living.

I walked out with my jacket over one shoulder, and 121 sticky dollars in my pocket. I felt pretty good walking back into Scott's Cafe. Of course I lost two hundred dollars to a bailiff a week later because I hadnt finished paying for the Austin.

I should have stayed home using one finger on my left hand to work on my novel. I had been working on it for a year or so, but did not want to write the last chapter. I would let four years go by before writing that last chapter. Someone gets killed. Meanwhile, I was learning how to write poems, and more important, poetics, mainly domestic versions of William Carlos Williams and Charles Olson. I sat coolly and cared for the syllable. I got over an unfortunate weakness for jazzy rhetoric.

I was a journalist, too, dont forget. I took Angela Luoma to hear Cannonball Adderly's sextet with Yusef Lateef, because I had to review the music for the *Ubyssey* critics' pages. I took notes with my left hand and tried to hold my cigarette with the two straight fingers sticking out of the redolent cast.

But for some reason I came home by myself on the night

of October 6. I had probably gone on one of my old-time pub crawls, or a shortened version that did not carry me as far east as the Princeton Hotel. I do, despite the fact that I was too drunk to drive a 1954 Austin, remember trying to get into my linoleumated False Creek digs that night. It was dark. It was raining a straight-down rain. I was carrying twelve bottles of Old Style Pilsener hanging from my two fingers, now as bent as the others. I could not find my front door key. I looked through every pocket, as one will do, three times, with my left hand.

Maybe Will was home. It was about three in the morning, if you can call anything morning above the False Creek warehouses in the rain. Will's girlfriend had to work weekends. He was probably sleeping in the little front room. I thought you were supposed to do the following to wake up a girlfriend, but things are different in the rain when you're between drunk and hungover. I could throw a stone that high with my left hand, I told myself. The streets are really steep above False Creek, so a second-storey window is pretty high. I started pegging little stones. They got harder and harder to find. I had to keep walking to the streetlight at the corner. Some rattled down the bent creosote shingles below our windows. Some hit nothing but trees and automobiles. But some snapped on a windowpane.

You know what a stone against your windowpane sounds like when you're inside—it's really loud. Especially at three in the morning. But I looked at the dark window for Will's scruffle-haired head, in vain. I would have to use the so-called fire escape. The so-called fire escape was a ladder nailed to the side of the house. If it were possible to get two storeys up on that ladder, I would find a little flat roof covered with warped asphalt shingles outside our little kitchen window. This was the window favoured by two cats we called Meredith and Phyllis.

I did not think that I could make it up that ladder

with its rungs so close to the ugly green wall, black wall now in the 3:30 A.M. rain. It was raining persistently, and my eyeglasses were opaque with rain. I was still drunk, or angry enough to make up for whatever sobering I had suffered. I was carrying a dozen Pils. I thought of drinking a couple to lighten the load, but I could not think of a way to open them. I had to decide what to do with the two bent fingers protruding from the wet and soiled cast around my aching hand. Should I hang the case of beer from them, or use them to support my 180 pounds (counting the beer)? And how would I reach for the next rung without falling? How do I get into these situations? I asked, as usual.

Now I am trying to remember how I got up there, and I simply cannot, can hardly believe that I did. Getting the kitchen window open was a little problem—it stuck and rattled, but the sill was rotted like a rain-forest floor, and it would always open eventually.

I got in. Then I put the case of beer into the refrigerator, moving some sushi to make room. Then I snapped on the kitchen light and looked into the front room, where I saw Will's puzzling shape under a dark blanket. There were no blinds on any of our windows in any of our three rooms. Feeble light fell out of the rainy sky. Dawn would be late and grey.

"I'm home safe and sound," I said quietly.

"Jeeze, Cap'n," he said. "That horrible kid upstairs has been dropping marbles on the floor and out their window on that little roof. What time is it? How do I get any sleep around here?"

I closed the door to the front room.

Then, with soaked hair on my forehead, I sat down at the kitchen table and wrote my poem "Grandfather." I have not lately seen the manuscript, so I dont know whether I wrote it with my left hand or the aching fingers sticking out from my smelly cast. Then I went to my bed in the side room.

When I got up that afternoon it had stopped raining. Will was gone, probably to get sushi at his girlfriend's. Meredith and Phyllis were at the window. I let them in and gave them some of the oldest raw fish and rice. Outside every piece of nature and rotted fence was silver. There was almost a whole cup of coffee in the pot on the leaking gas stove. I had a bad pain right back of my forehead. I was still emotional but prepared to forgive Will when he blundered through the door.

We went through our usual comic routine, and then he told me that my grandfather poem was the best thing I'd ever written. He had known my grandfather, an old man with bad feet and a British vocabulary.

"What are you talking about?" I inquired. "This thing ignores or violates all the poetic principles that I have been working out these last two years."

"It's really good," he said.

Maybe it is, I thought.

"No, it's all that's wrong with poetry," I said.

Will was studying Japanese. He didnt know anything about poetics.

Still, I published the poem in *Tish* 14, along with a review of Jack Kerouac's *Big Sur*, a book that ends with a long poem a lot different from my short one. "Grandfather" would show up in my first book in 1964, and would appear in all my selected volumes, I think. And it would show up in lots and lots of anthologies, including all those anthologies created for colleges and high schools. It's a "teachable poem," I guess, and thus confirms the reservations I expressed about it when it was less than one day old. Those editors must have agreed with my roommate.

I guess all the poets in Canada were writing poems about their grandfathers in those days. At least the male poets were. I dont remember all that many grandmother poems, although I wrote one that didnt get into the anthologies. Grandfather poems were good for the thematic nationalists of the sixties and seventies, and are probably good for their successors, the identity post-colonialists of the nineties. Those old relatives got called things like "prairie patriarchs." They were pioneers of a "national literature," or something like that. They were examples used in essays that employed the adjective "cultural."

Part of the reason that my "Grandfather" was so rhetorical is that my grandfather (he was never called "Jabez" in the family) was a circuit rider in Manitoba and Alberta. I never heard him preach, but I wanted some Baptist noise in the poem. Besides, I was wet and drunkish, and my hand was killing me.

The anthologists made their selections from other anthologies. For years I claimed that I made more from the poem than my grandfather made as a circuit rider around Pilot Mound and Wetaskiwin.

I never even went to church with him. When my grandmother was alive I went with her to the Baptist church in West Summerland, B.C. At home in Oliver, I went to Sunday school in the United church. There was no Baptist church in Oliver. In West Summerland with my grandmother I heard the choir and everyone else singing "Holy holy holy, Lord God Almighty." It seemed to bulge the walls a little. The song ended "God in three persons, blessed Trinity." I didnt have a clue what that meant, but it sounded great, and I figured that that's why you would sing "holy" three times. I also knew that the line wouldnt have worked with two of them or four of them. My grandmother did not know that she was taking me to a poetry lesson.

I remember two reading experiences with her. She disapproved of a book I was reading: *The Gashouse Gang*. She had no idea that it was about the St. Louis Cardinals of the thirties. Her favourite comic strip was *Little Orphan Annie*. She would read it out loud to me. When the gangsters said "yeah," she read it as "yea." I expected a "verily." I never had the nerve to ask her how she understood that narrative.

There came a time when Allen Ginsberg did not want to read *Howl* to audiences any more, and I know my own little version of what he meant. After a while I would not read my grandfather poem, despite its rhetorical nature, or because of it. Or because, despite the anthologies, I did not relish being a one-trick peony.

Besides, it became embarrassing to recite the errors in the poem, or warn about them before reading it. If you understand poems as linguistic events, they dont have errors in them, but if you read the short handwritten autobiography my grandfather wrote in his last days, you knew that the poem could use a little revision. (It is going to get some, but not because of the errors.)

For one thing, the child who would become my grand-dad did not take an Anabaptist cane across his back every day. I dont think that I even knew what an Anabaptist was when I angrily wrote the poem. According to my granddad's autobiography, he was a normal Church of England orphan. In fact, his sister would become a Church of England nun. He became a Baptist (not an Anabaptist) when he found out that he had lost an argument about religion with the farm couple who employed him as an (almost) indentured labourer in Manitoba. He converted, and soon decided to go to divinity school and become a Baptist preacher. So my father's father was not an Anabaptist, but my mother's mother was. Born in Michigan, she was a Mennonite girl, whose family had moved from Oregon to Alberta, where she and her sister married Baptist brothers who had moved there from the Ozarks.

When my granddad and his brother came from England to Canada, they came first to Quebec, not the Ontario of the poem; and when my preacher grandfather moved from Manitoba to Alberta, it was not via Saskatchewan that he travelled, but rather through Minnesota, where he was a circuit rider north of Minneapolis. He was all set to take employment in Idaho, when the Church asked him to go to work south of Edmonton, where the Lutherans were snapping up too many of the available young believers.

But that's just political geography. He wound up living with my parents after his second wife Clara died, my father Ewart being the dutiful son, I guess. We built another addition to the house. I got my middle name from my granddad, as did my father. As for the Catholic hospital in Oliver, B.C., it was the only hospital between Penticton and the border. It was a block from our house. My father was the most energetic organizer in the creation of the new secular hospital. A couple years ago the beautiful old one was torn down to make room for condominiums. My grandfather took classical languages at divinity school, but he never heard that word.

Coming to Shelley

I N THE SUMMER OF 1963, when all the famous poets were in Vancouver for their famous poetry convention, I had been planning to spend all my time within earshot of Charles Olson, who was in those days the standard-bearer for the kind of poetry my friends and I were planning to live our lives in. I did see quite a lot of Olson, and heard his marvellous seven-hour poetry reading, all those *Maximus* poems that had not yet been published. But then my ear was seized by another poet—or I should say two poets.

For Allen Ginsberg, just back from his sojourn in Asia, his hair hanging curly from the back of his head, opened his East-disciplined throat and recited two oracular poems that I had always known of and always ignored because they did not align themselves easily with the poetry I had chosen to follow, which was written by Ezra Pound and William Carlos Williams.

One day in the park Ginsberg recited "Ode to the West Wind" by Percy Bysshe Shelley. A few days later, somewhere on the green green campus of the University of British Columbia, he recited all of "Adonais" by the same poet. I was electrified. I had felt an honest-to-God *aura* around the person of Allen. Now I felt the beginning of a complete change in my poetry direction.

Ezra Pound had somehow persuaded me that the Romantics were "sludge," even if he was talking about the worst imitators. If we young poets were anything, we were loyal to our cabals. I fall upon the thorns of life, I bleed, spoke some high school English teacher, not in the habit of reading poetry at home. I thought of the romantic poet putting the back of his wrist to his forehead and intoning a poem filled with abstract words denoting passion between the tubercular coughs that presaged fame.

But Ginsberg nearly shouted those poems, his whole body proffered to the air that seemed almost to recoil from his assault. I knew instantly that Ginsberg was right about Shelley—the power is there, I heard—and I knew that I would start poetry all over again, with Shelley on the first page.

Three years later I was in the Vale of Chamonix, staring at the bright snow on Mont Blanc. I was in Europe for the first time in my life, on a six-week voyage from London to Istanbul. A year before, a passenger jet had crashed on Mont Blanc. A while later a gondola lift had come apart, spilling human bodies on the snowy slope. A reader looking at the late May snow did not have to be further instructed about the power that would reside there. The cave of the witch Poesie was not a languid trope. By now, the reader knew that the everlasting universe of things rolls through the mind.

When I returned home at the end of the summer I opened a book I had never seen before, and saw that Shelley wrote a journal of a six-week voyage that took him to Chamonix in 1616, exactly 150 years before.

In the autumn of 1966 I enrolled in a seminar on Shelley and Keats with Ross Woodman at the University of Western Ontario. Woodman was an inspirational interpreter of English Romantic poetry, and in his seminar I learned to respect Shelley's acute intelligence, his tireless appetite for knowledge that would be fed into his total devotion to the spirit of poetry and social revolution. Far from the pallid aesthete I had fancied him to be, Shelley turned out to be the most rigorous mind in English poetry. He also wrote excellent poems in every verse poem that had been invented. He was a terrifyingly *serious* poet who both lived and died for his art, and who accomplished the seeming paradox: he was a skeptical Platonist at the same time that he believed in a Perfectibility that must be seen in the liberation and education of the mortal human.

Any poet, it seems to me, will find such a model precursor, and try to live up to him or her, all the time admitting in rue and pleasure that he will never achieve such a feat. I still try to put myself into the presence of Charles Olson by opening his big poem. I will always be thankful to Allen Ginsberg for reciting those two great poems. And I will never stop looking up to that man Shelley, who died when he was the age I had attained when I heard his words from Allen's throat.

The Ryerson Split

I N 1966 I TOOK A DEEP breath and moved east, to London, Ontario. I was at the beginning of my writing career, and London was close to Toronto, where the publishers and broadcasters were. My first novel had been accepted by McClelland & Stewart, I had been on a few television programs (yes, in those days Canadian television was interested in literature), and now I had a story in a fiction anthology published by one of the country's biggest Toronto publishers, Ryerson Press.

The anthology was *Modern Canadian Stories*. My story was at the back because I was so young. The editors were Giose Rimanelli and Roberto Ruberto. Other stories were by people even I had heard of—Morley Callaghan and Hugh Garner and Margaret Laurence. I really felt as if I were going places. I didnt feel too badly about spending ten dollars on a pair of stretch-material slightly bell-bottomed pants I had bought in Düsseldorf on my six-dollar-a-day trip to Europe in the summer.

Things could hardly be more exciting. Ryerson Press threw a reception for the anthology in some hotel meeting room right in the middle of probably storied literary Toronto.

People told me that this was a rare event, because Ryerson was the United Church and they didnt usually look kindly on the idea of literary bunfights with alcoholic drinks. I didnt know then and I dont know now whether these people were serious or whether they were just misleading the western fellow with their practised irony. Anyway, I could remember the summer poetry festival at UBC in 1963. There Ryerson had provided a half-hour's worth of Canadian wine or something, and Jack Spicer and I had liberated a couple bottles and carried them across some flower beds to a well-lit parking lot.

Anyway, here I was three and a half years later, a minor but promising literary figure in a room in Toronto, watching writers who obviously knew each other talk to each other. Thank goodness, I thought, that Earle Birney and Phyllis Webb were there. I knew them both from Vancouver. Earle had been extremely kind to Angela and me here in our first year of the East, throwing a party for us, and introducing me to literary types. Phyllis was working for the CBC, and she had included me in both television and radio productions.

The editors were there, being extremely Italian in their suits. I saw Morley Callaghan, who looked tremendously old, which was to be expected by 1966. He had a red face and was wearing a whiplash cushion around his neck. Hugh Garner also had a red face. He was sitting at a table of little sandwiches and pickles, drinking alcohol and telling stories fairly loudly in a raspy voice. Boy, literary figures, I thought to myself.

The party had just begun. Nevertheless, I dropped a napkin on the floor. When I bent to pick it up my German pants stopped stretching and ripped from beginning to middle to end. It was a story I didnt want to hear. I hadnt even had a second drink yet, those nice high drinks in those nice hotel glasses. I hadnt eaten any free food yet. I hadnt had a talk with any writers or even Barbara Amiel yet. Damn, I said to my writerly self.

I couldnt leave this early, I thought. I got myself a plate full of little sandwiches and pickles and sat down on my rip with the white shorts inside, and talked for a while with Phyllis Webb. That was okay, but I was getting more and more nervous. I told Earle Birney about my problem. He said he would lend me a pair of his pants. But my own pants were black and stretchy and skin-tight. What would Earle's probably baggy pants with short legs look like? I said no thank you, not because I didnt want Earle's pants, but because I was enraged at my bad western-boy luck.

My first Toronto literary reception.

No one from the Toronto *Telegram* had even got to me yet. Who knew when Ryerson would spring for alcohol again?

I wish now that I had worn Earle's pants. I wish I had just borrowed a safety pin.

As it was, I resolved to pick my Toronto career up again when given another chance. For now I would just have to get my 1954 Chevrolet, parked seven blocks away where the closest free parking was, that is behind Coach House Press, and head for the 401 to London. The cold wind and probably some of the wind-driven snow found its way to my nether smile. I was stamping on the snow-drifted sidewalks.

I had only one drink in me. I could drive the 401 as fast as the snow would let me. It was two and a half hours to London, in the Ontario dark. I listened to the radio and then I listened to the tires on the highway. My sense of humour did not arrive.

Twenty miles short of London there was a sudden bang, and then a continued metallic noise. The car slowed down, and I thought I might have to park there beside the road, in the dark, under the invisible cloud bank that was hiding the winter stars. But whatever it was allowed me to drive slowly along the shoulder of the highway until I got to a garage. There I heard that I had experienced that event spoken of so much in company I used to keep—I had thrown a rod. I did not then, nor do I now, know what that means.

Except that I had to get a ride into London and then think of what I was going to do with that Chevrolet parked twenty miles toward literary Toronto. The guy in the garage did not ask me about the rip in my trousers. Maybe it wasnt noticeable.

Writing About British Columbia

A T SOUTHERN OKANAGAN High School, if you were in the A classes you had to take two majors. There wasnt a lot of choice, because this was not one of your big schools down at the Coast. So I majored in English and social studies, and then I said what the heck and took a third major in math. We got report cards three times a year. In my report card someone always wrote that I was not working up to my capability. Once, in grade nine, I got an A in something in my second report, which came in February, I think. It was probably in social studies, which was mainly history, as far as I could see. I buckled down and made sure that that A disappeared before June. In six years of high school I never did get an A on a final report card. How could I? My father was a science teacher at SOHS. I strived to remain a C-plus student.

When I got to university I found out that you could take one major or two majors, so I took two. I got my B.A. in creative writing and history, which meant that I took the bare minimum of the latter, including a course on Japanese history. One day I wrote a three-hour exam in U.S. history and then raced across the UBC campus and took a three-hour exam in U.S. literature.

Then I decided to do an M.A. in English. Although I had taken a lot of esoteric English courses to find stuff out, I didnt have the right undergraduate courses, so I was an "unclassified" student for a year. It was my favourite year in my eighteen years of school. All I took were English courses: Chaucer and Shakespeare and eighteenth century and so on. I also wrote a novel and lots of poems and columns for the Oliver newspaper and the UBC newspaper, and tutored Hungarian immigrants in English and acted in plays and worked on the UBC literary magazine. What a neat year. But for the first time I was not taking history.

Then I did my M.A. in English, which included a bullshit creative writing thesis, and then I went and taught at Calgary for three years, and then went and enrolled at Western Ontario as a Ph.D. student, and the rest—well, the rest is not history, but it has always seemed to involve history.

While at Western I started a history-based poem on the voyages of Captain George Vancouver. In the following years I wrote more long poems dealing with history, and pretty soon I was writing a series of historical novels. Why the hell am I doing this? I wondered. I always said that I wrote history stuff because I didnt know any history and wanted to learn some. It took me a while to suspect that I had known what was coming when I took a B.A. in creative writing and history. I had never thought that I was doing either.

After trying to market some of my historical novels, Penguin Books badgered me to write some "real" history. By "real" history they meant amateur history. So I wrote two long amateur histories. The first one was a history of British Columbia. The reviewers liked it, and many strangers wrote to tell me how much they and their fathers liked it. They said that they were really glad to find out so much about British Columbia. I was the voice of British Columbia, they said.

I dont think that I am quintessentially British Columbian, but I am probably typically British Columbian in various ways. For instance, I find myself aligning with B.C. against Back East in various confrontations. As a writer, I suppose I have a predilection for marginal writing, and I think that over most of our history, there have been more unconventional writers in B.C. than you'd find elsewhere, far more than there are in Nova Scotia, some more than in Ontario.

As a person reared in the Okanagan, I, of course, feel

doubly or triply marginalized. I was from Canada, not the U.S., from B.C., not Ontario/Quebec, and Okanagan, not Coast. So I had an inferiority complex, an invaluable asset when it comes to researching and writing books.

My wife Angela came out of that Finnish community on Quadra Island. Then she went to school in Courtenay, living in various communities in that place that the locals call the Comox Valley, though it doesnt look like a valley to me. The Finns were loggers: that's two kinds of strange people. Angela was created with a lot of Finn in her, I'll tell you.

But in the early days of our marriage we lived in Alberta and Ontario and Quebec. I was becoming more and more Canadian, and found myself sometimes defending Canadian (or Quebec) ideas against West Coast attitudes. In terms of literature, I was always telling West Coast people to pay more attention to eastern stuff, and telling easterners to pay more attention to B.C. stuff. I was always finding myself pulled both ways. Sort of like British Columbia itself, the province of communist fishermen and knuckle-dragging right-wing school boards.

I dont think that I would use the term "schizophrenic," though I understand that popular usage. Yes, I have heard a similar view of Oregon, where they would elect a right-winger to State Senate, and send a quasi-socialist to Washington. All my life I have seen that there are two political parties in B.C.: the social democrats and the anti-social democrats, whatever they call themselves for the nonce.

The surface of the B.C. character keeps changing, but there is always a kind of continuity. While I was writing my book I kept noticing current matters that resembled stuff that happened a hundred years ago. In terms of anti-Asian racism, we used to complain that poor Chinese were coming in and taking jobs; more recently we complain that rich Chinese are coming in and taking real estate.

When I lived back east, even I had trouble understanding

B.C. Maybe I was becoming more ordinary, more Canadian, more mainstream. Maybe I was losing my identification as an underground writer. Writing the B.C. history twenty-five years later seemed more aboveground than just about anything else I have written. In fact, I really enjoyed upbraiding family members and others for being ignorant of something I had just found out a week before. It made me feel like the responsible citizen.

As a veteran of somewhat unconventional historical novels, I was highly aware that I was in a position to plant a few new historical weeds. It was an awesome responsibility to stick to the facts. I will never forget Henry James's insistence that both the novelist and the historian owe it to their readers to represent reality. Actually, I was so faithful that there were times when I was worried that I was being overly straitlaced. Well....

In the last historical novel before writing *Bowering's B.C.*, I was trying to cleave more closely to history than I had in the previous ones, or at least to cut down on the disrespectful humour. It was about some half-Indian brothers who were finally hanged by the white man's government. *The Wild McLeans* was my working title, but Mel Rothenburger got to it first, so I called my second western *Shoot!* Then I find out that it was the title of a novel by Pirandello.

A lot of people noted the differences between my westerns and the normal U.S. ones. The U.S. American West was tamer than the novels and movies that portrayed it. But we did have a quieter time of it, in terms of the prior inhabitants. We did not get the army to ride into villages and kill the population. We did have a first governor who had killed non-combatants, though.

I think that I have always been good at titles, but when it came to my history books I had a hell of a time coming up with a good title. Then I had titles thrust on me. I didnt too much like *Bowering's B.C.*, and I was not taken by the subtitle

A Swashbuckling History. I have never cared for the term "swashbuckling" here. I always associate it with pirate movies. I have never buckled a swash. I have knuckled a squash, but that was back in the Okanagan.

After writing so much historical fiction, I was used to doing research, and in fact research is in some ways my favourite part of doing a book. But now that I was writing a "real" history I was afraid that I was being a little dry. I often had the feeling that I was not fooling around enough with language. My publisher Cynthia Good told me right from the beginning that they wanted my kind of writing, and that's why they used that title. I did stay away from the first-person almost all of the time, though.

I was not prepared for the favourable reviews. Some of them were embarrassingly favourable. I thought I knew what was going to happen regarding reviews, if any. Newspapers would send the book to history professors. I do sometimes get bothered by reviews and articles, but I would never write one of those pained-author letters to the book review editor. When I write history books I just want W. Kaye Lamb to love me.

I am glad that my first "real" history book was about my home province. I am just sorry that my home province did not send more prime ministers to Ottawa for my second "real" history book. The historian's job is made pleasurable by the fact that B.C. has usually had some kind of whacko for premier. A lawyer with grey hair doesnt have much of a chance to preside in Victoria. High school dropouts have been favoured by the Socreds and their successors, the Reform party. B.C. voters have often shown that they will try something new—a fat guy in a silk hat, a Maritimer with a made-up name. Glen Clark proved that the voters will elect two guys with bad moustaches in a row.

Somehow the inherent goofiness of B.C. politics did not

appeal much to previous historians. Margaret Ormsby's big book arrived for one of our centenaries, in 1958, and it justifiably became the standard history. Here is a good reason: in 1955 Bruce Alistair McKelvie, acclaimed in the B.C. legislature "the foremost historian of the Province," published *Pageant of B.C.*, in which he maintained that Coast Indian customs show the influence of early Chinese Jewish explorers. Dr. Ormsby's book perhaps shows the givens of the fifties: her first chapter is about the European approaches from the sea, and her second chapter is about the European approaches from the Prairies. My book starts a little earlier in time.

The histories by Jean Barman and George Woodcock certainly take angles not considered by Ormsby. But when I looked in either index I did not find the McLean brothers, and all Joe Fortes got was a passing mention in a compound sentence in Barman's book. I think that their stories are as important as the stories of John Oliver and Emily Carr. Woodcock's anarchism did not influence me, but I admired it. I always agreed with Woodcock (and Ethel Wilson) that one might be a B.C. person before being a Canadian.

But, as I said, the research was a lot more interesting than reading previous histories. As I am not a real historian, I did not spend a billion hours unearthing original stuff that had never come to light before. But I read stuff that I would normally never pick up: books about the wine business, local histories self-published by old-timers, guides for nineteenth-century immigrants.

I admire Barman's book because it included thorough examinations of various parts of human life, telling about education, women's lives, the arts, and so on. The style is professorial, though. Robin Fisher's *Contact and Conflict* is interesting because it goes into complex detail concerning the effects on native life of the European arrivals. I really liked the tone of Martin Robin's *The Company Province*. And I want to recommend the publications of the En'owkin Centre in Penticton, the native education headquarters for the province and the country.

I was struck by how late the idea of literature came to B.C. Then I was struck by how long the practices of poetry and narrative had been there. Mr. Robert Bringhurst changed my notion of B.C. literature a few years ago, when he used the term to include native stories.

It was interesting to read poetry and fiction that you could not call "literature" in the evaluative sense. Books can be interesting for various reasons. It can be a hoot to read terrible verses pencilled in boom towns of the North. David Corcoran's *The West Coasters* had me turning pages to see what was going to happen to his characters mingling with historical figures in the late nineteenth century. But the book is a romance. Its author wanted it to be one of those blockbusters, and the writing is pitched at people sitting in airplanes. If we are talking about literature, and I am, I'll stay with Daphne Marlatt's novel *Ana Historic*. It offers a sharp re-creation of late nineteenth-century Burrard Inlet, but it does not make things easy for the tourists.

A theme that pervades my book is the insistence of racism since the coming of the miners from the south. I do not know how anyone could read about B.C.'s treatment of native land since the gold rush and not lean a long way over toward the First Nations' view. When I see people holding signs that urge "One people, one law," I want to ask them where they were when Indians could not vote, or when the B.C. government "gave" the people less than half the land that the federal government mandated. The admirable Nisga'a people have been trying to correct miserable treatment for well over a century.

I did not know the all-pervasive influence of racism in

just about every aspect of our lives in this province. In the early twentieth century the politicians ran on competitive anti-Asian platforms. The first action of the Royal Canadian Navy was taken against British subjects who were from the Punjab. The first unions in the province fought management about non-white workers. Citizens are voting the race ticket all over the province today.

People often ask me my opinion regarding the most livable place in the province. I wont tell you the best place to live because then the readers will turn it into another Kelowna. When I was a kid, Kelowna was a lovely little city on the lake, and there were weeping willows in everyone's yard. Then an eastern businessman named Bennett came to town, and then Bennett's party got a superhighway built between Kelowna and the Coast. Now Kelowna is a shopping mall with its parking lots full of sports utility vehicles.

The worst place to live in B.C.? Next to any 7-Eleven store, especially when school is in.

Doing It Right on the Inside of Town

WHEN I WAS TWENTY-ONE YEARS OLD, fresh and pseudo-sophisticated out of the air force, I came down out of the mountains to the university and the big city. Three or four days a week I hung out at campus, stepping on romantic wet maple leaves and reading Albert Camus as fast as I could. On the other days and all through the nights I was downtown, walking with hunched shoulders beneath the rain-blurred neon lights, looking for "material."

By day I was a university student. By night I was a young novelist. You could not get a beer anywhere but downtown in those days. You could not get a university education anywhere but out on the nose of Point Grey. The only real urban education you were likely to get was in the Chili Bowl Cafe on Main Street about three in the morning.

I think I was living in a couple of movies. They were both escape entertainment. Downtown was an escape from the academic life, and the university was a refuge from the grit and honk of the city core. It seemed as if I should have been carrying a passport all the time, or a ticket.

Maybe we were buying into an old North American idea of a university. It should be basically an agriculture college out in the country. Or it should be a rural repose where divinity students would not be tempted by the whizz of the metropolis. Certainly those were the alternatives for whatever members of my family made their way to post-secondary learning.

But there had always been the other concept. Universities, after all, had from earliest times sprung up a block or two from the centres of trade. Plato had travelled all over the Greek world, but he set up the Academy in downtown Athens. Galileo taught in a university right smack in the middle of Padua. He could pop out for a beer with his business friends right after teaching his last physics class in the afternoon. These days the University of Paris has campuses all over the city, and you can reach most of them by subway.

When Simon Fraser University was dreamed up and then blueprinted, the idea was that it would serve the lower mainland, but that it would also reach out for those students who did not have the kind of life in which it was convenient to sit down for four years of solid book-banging. You should be able to fit a few courses into a schedule that was already looking like a sack full of rocks—job, children, volunteer program, lunch on the art gallery steps. In other words, you should not have to quit getting a university education just because the only campus was a movie set surrounded by trees somewhere out beyond the bus lines.

Well, they built Simon Fraser University on a bare spot hacked out of the trees on top of a "mountain" overlooking the distant harbour. Something had to be done, the sensible people said. We cannot abandon those downtown citizens to whatever they can learn in a Teflon-topped stadium. Two things seemed necessary: night classes and downtown classes. Exactly, I said. I had taught mostly night classes at Sir George Williams University in the middle of Montreal.

So they found a downtown building they could share, and slotted night classes into it. I taught some of those classes. They were in a tall thin building with no windows, twenty blocks from the nearest coffee shop. No fun. Once a week someone would pull the fire alarm and we all had to walk down seven flights of stairs, surrounded by blotchy concrete. Plato would have left for Sicily.

But now we have the magnificent site you can read all about in the expensive-looking advertisement brochures the university doesnt mind paying for. Urban education now means at least two things: you can continue your university experience at the traditional main intersection of Canada's prettiest rainy city, and while you are there you can take courses on what it means to be an urban citizen. If you dont look out, I may be teaching one of them.

And if you are going to be a novelist? Well, the Chili Bowl Cafe has been gone for years, but there are lots of Galileos sitting at friendly tables not too many steps in any direction from the classroom. It might even be part of your education to drop a few with them.

WRITING BASEBALL

Baseball Has Been Very Good to Me

VANCOUVER PEOPLE DONT like being inside the house. As I sit inside my house on any early February day, wondering whether I can wait another two weeks to get out on the ball field, I cast my mind back three months to the last time I was out on the ball field. Oh, the mind is a wonderful thing. The body, on the other hand, leaves something to be desired.

That's not quite right. I think I have seen a few bodies that bring the idea of desire up. Let's say that *my* body leaves something to be desired. At least for someone who has to live inside it. Living inside this body, which I have done, incidentally, for well more than half a century, keeps me in touch with last summer. Let's be more specific: with last ball season.

For instance, my left hand. Sometimes I bang my left hand against a door jamb, and then I say something in a theological manner. This is because one July I got my left hand broken by a moron who kept running instead of sliding while he was trying to steal second base. A large moron. I got a perfect throw from our catcher and the large moron ran his leg bones right into the tag. I knew my hand was broken, but I figured shock would make everything all right till after the game. Next two times up I bunted and drew a walk. But in the last inning we had the winning run on base, so I bit down hard on my imitation chewing tobacco and hit a liner over the drawn-in left fielder. We won and I drove to the university hospital. "You again?" asked the admitting nurse.

I also have a dark thing that used to be a bruise and is now a scar on my right knee. That's from the diving stab at a grounder I didnt make in the same game, an inning after I broke the hand that was now pretty snug in my glove.

Over the years on Vancouver ball diamonds I have broken a toe and a nose and a wrist and a cheekbone. I've got a concussion during the annual New Year's Day game. I've had a bruise that ran from my knee down to my foot and up to my pain threshold. I have glaucoma in both eyes after line drives administered there. Baseball's been very good to me.

That's why I long for summer. In summer the sun shines and the puddle disappears from the batter's box, and that familiar phrase rings out across the park: "Did you bring the Ben-Gay?"

I remember the summer and I long for the next one, but even I will admit that I am not really in the summer of my life. For years now people have been telling me I'm too old to play ball. My family tells me that. My own team tells me that. Once a bookstore clerk I had never met before told me that.

But my hero is the Mexican mural painter David Alfaro Siqueiros. The Mexican government jailed and exiled him seven times for being a leftist activist. The last time they let him out he was sixty-five years old. There were four thousand people waiting outside the prison. They had already rented the biggest theatre in Mexico City for the celebration and fiery speeches. The official release time was noon. But this was summer. Siqueiros said he wasnt coming out till the game was over. He was a sixty-five-year-old first baseman, and his team was in the pennant race.

I'm the oldest guy in my league now, and I always did run the bases like a sewing machine. But I make up in savvy what I dont have in acceleration. In February the trunk of my Volvo is already loaded down with bats and balls and gloves and Neat's Foot Oil and batting gloves and baseball hats and a catcher's mask. Until it got broken, I even added a deck chair, one of the retirement presents my team buys me at the end of every season.

No, no, I didnt say rocking chair.

And I bought a new Rawlings Spin-Stopper bat. It cost me more than I told my wife, and it's top quality. It'll be good for years.

Baseball and Bile

ONCE IN A WHILE YOU GET pointedly reminded of your mortality, and your first thought is always: Have I played my last ball game?

For a few months I had been having those dark yellow pees, and sometimes over the month previous to all this I had the kind of high abdomen pains we all cheerily call heartburn. Then, fittingly, while I was at a Vancouver Canadians baseball game with my friend Doug I ate a whole huge bag of unshelled peanuts, a hot dog with darn near everything on it, including sauerkraut, and three beers. At ball games I usually have 0–1 beers. In the eighth inning I started getting an attack, and I actually left the park with only one out in the ninth inning! I drove home and felt the attack getting worse. At one o'clock in the morning I got a ride to Vancouver General Hospital in an ambulance, and there finished the eight hours of an awful pain. I dont recommend it.

So then I started not eating and, yes, going to doctors. Dr. Campana in Emergency had bet on gall bladder. Dr. Perlman, our family doc, guessed hiatus hernia, and sent me for ultrasound at VGH, which I went to. They couldnt find anything in my gall bladder, but they saw that my bile duct was dilated. Dr. Perlman sent me to Dr. Carr, a digestion specialist, and quite well known—wasnt that a break? He said I was jaundiced, and called Dr. Perlman and said I had to be admitted. So on the Friday I went in, six days after the big attack. I'd had a medium-big attack Tuesday, the day of the ultrasound, because I ate two meals the day before.

I got out Sunday to DH in our ball game, and went two for five. Then they did X-rays on Monday. And then more ultrasound, with six of the radiologists puzzled for hours. They were going to do my procedure on Tuesday, but I think I got bumped for a more important patient. Anyway, I languished till Thursday, late afternoon, reading some, watching Seattle baseball games on an expensive little rented earphone TV. Angela got there just in time on Thursday to accompany me to the operating room.

What they had was an X-ray table, and a tube they stick down your throat and digestive system, and it has a camera and sharp little knife on the end of it, as well as a little light bulb and a basket. You look, if you are the gastronomist, you cut, and you retrieve. They said that in the bile duct there might be stones or tumours, let's look. I had a lot of black-ish thoughts that week. When I came to, being gurneyed out, I was groggily aware of Angela saying, "No tumour." There was no stone either. Two weeks later there was still a dilated duct. There were a lot of blood vessels down there. Not much risk but some, advised Dr. Carr. I thought, as I know others did, of bp, our lovely lost.

My body didnt look very yellow to me the next Monday, but my eyes still were. I got out of the hospital Friday evening. On Sunday I went two for six. But I had lost seventeen pounds, and so did not hit a home run. It was a great pleasure to eat food you have to chew, after having only four clear fluids for two weeks. If you want to try to lose seventeen pounds, try clear fluids.

Now there was a chance of liver you-know-what, but we are saying nah. Also I would have to have another tube down into my stomach the following week. I got a little behind in things, but started a new poem series, a short and not very good one, while in hospital. The guy kitty-corner from me in my room, 689W, was younger and worse off than I. You could smell his innards, and he said that he had not eaten anything in two years.

In the hospital it was exciting to wake up because just outside my open window, they were building a new pavil-ion of the VGH, all out of steel, and at 6:45 every morning except the weekend, there was a loud clanging that woke you up wondering whether you had made it through the night....

Eventually I got out of the hospital, and was told not to play ball for the rest of the year. Are you kidding? I compromised by DHing and playing only an inning at second base. And there was professional baseball to keep up with, though I would not carry a king-sized bag of peanuts to any park with me any more.

My travel agent screwed up my trip to a poetry bash in Minneapolis. I told her I was going there early so that I could see the Blue Jays game at the Hump on September 13 at noon, and she made up my ticket, on weird airlines, for that day, so that when I get there I had to lug my suitcase to the stadium in order to catch the last two innings. How wonderful. I had so looked forward and indeed bragged about seeing a game in another stadium I hadnt previously visited. I had made it to Cleveland the year before. That is such a wonderful hobby. I collect a number of things: university T-shirts, foreign editions of *On the Road*, and baseball stadiums.

The best one I ever sat in was Tiger Stadium in Detroit. The worst was windy frozen Candlestick Park in San Francisco. But I would rather sit in a sleeping bag at hoodlum-infested Candlestick Park than lie there beside the clanging at Vancouver General Hospital.

Diamonds, Not Rhinestones

J TAKE A BOOK WITH ME TO the ball park. The loudest cheers go up around me while I'm reading a Japanese short story. People are cheering three plywood horses' heads outside the left-field fence, racing for the foul pole while the PA person makes like the announcer at the track. Minor league stuff; in Toronto it's three airplanes on the Jumbo Tron.

The bad news is that the Major League Baseball Association, conscious of the fact that professional basketball is now the big deal, and worried about fan-fallaway, is planning more circus and less bread. Millionaire ballplayers engaged in labour grievances and the trading of really good players who can make more money elsewhere tend to make a fan's identification with his heroes difficult. When Larry Walker laughed off a suspension because it cost him only three days' pay—$100,000, some folks noticed that that was more than they make in a year.

Recently the major leagues created some more divisions and more playoffs. It is still not as bad as hockey, but it doesn't smell like baseball. Not to a fan who cares more about a double play than a Ken Griffey playing card.

Baseball's best writer was Ring Lardner. When I was a teenage baseball reporter and a confused young poet, I modelled myself on him. Seventy-five years ago Ring Lardner complained about the way business was widening the gap between the fans and the game. Trying to overcome the damage done by the Black Sox scandal in the 1919 World Series, major league baseball started the lively ball era, going for razzmatazz instead of the hit and run. I always loved the hit and run, and I feel smug knowing that most of the people around me at the ball park dont know what the hell it is.

Corporate team owners and Barry Bonds's salary are

probably going to do the game more harm than the Black Sox ever did, and no one today will ever hit as well as Shoeless Joe Jackson did. So how is the Major League Baseball Association going to get the fans back? They could stop thinking of them as warm bums in grandstand seats, and start thinking of those kids who keep a scribbler full of stats and wear their ball caps frontward. I snuck one of them into my novel *Caprice*, as a kind of secret message to my friends such as Clark Blaise. Clark would know what I was doing. Maybe the baseball business people could stop thinking about that disgusting word "marketing" for a minute, and think about why that kid in Chicago said, "Say it aint so, Joe!"

The Toronto Blue Jays have the idea of getting some of their players to give out free autographs once in a while. But why do they have to do it in a kiosk? A kiosk looks like something in marketing, something that would appeal to the sort of junior hoodlum who's planning on selling that autograph. Let the damned players sign autographs for the kids who are waiting at the stadium door after the game. So the air-conditioned bus has to wait a while. Give the driver a big raise or trade him to a team that will appreciate his talents.

I've got nothing against skydivers dropping onto the field, or special salutes to agriculture nights, with ballplayers milking cows. Baseball players and fans come from the sticks, anyway. But why does baseball have to act like the other pro sports? Turn down the volume and never mind the 3-D trading cards. Give us back our bloody intimacy. Maybe someone could figure out how to build a nice little ballpark inside SkyDome Trademark Registered.

Feller and the Sunsplash

T HERE WAS A LOT OF NOISE in the open square of the old market in Victoria. It was a summer's day, there were billions of American tourists in town, and this was a place where the heritage people felt a lot of pride. It looked like about as old as you can get on the West Coast, and at the same time it looked like the kind of place where no Winnebago rider would be afraid to browse for a frozen-yogurt cone.

The noise was coming from a band that was warming up some giant electronic speakers in the square. It was the middle of a long August weekend called Victoria Sunsplash, a combination of black music and hip poetry, and the brainchild of one Hope Anderson, black poet and semi-professional music promoter.

Yesterday Taj Mahal and his guitar and bongo had mellowed lots of listeners out in the buttery evening sun; and then in the twilight Amiri Baraka woke them up to their own bulging eyes and quivering ears as he laid down the fiercest lines of poetry ever heard in staid Empress Victoria. One was grateful to be there.

This day there will be a family of drummers from Senegal and a famous singing prince from the record jackets; but there is also a sign in the window of the sports store in the corner of the market square. The sign says that Bob Feller will be there to sign autographs.

You have to understand that 1948 was the greatest year in the history of human civilization, and that one of the most important things to happen in 1948 was that at last Bob Feller would get his chance to pitch in the World Series.

In 1948, if you were talking about singing, you said Sinatra. If you were talking about hitting, you probably said DiMaggio. But if the subject was pitching, you started and ended all discussions with the phrase "Bob Feller."

Bob Feller did get his chance to start in a World Series game. In fact, his Cleveland Indians beat the Boston Braves four games to two, and Feller started in the two games the Indians lost. Those losses, especially the loss in the opening game, formed the material for the sad-heart sports story of 1948.

Feller should have won that first game. He pitched a two-hitter, and lost 1–0 to Johnny Sain, the best pitcher in the National League. Moreover, the one run that crossed the plate had no business being there, and the proof was on hundreds of sports pages the following day and all the next winter. It is one of the most famous photographs in sports: Lou Boudreau laying the tag on the shoulder of Phil Masi, out by a foot and a half on Feller's great pickoff in the eighth inning. But National League umpire Bill Stewart called Masi safe, and he scored on the second Brave hit of the game.

It was a terrible shame. I was not a Cleveland fan. In fact, in 1948 the Indians beat my cherished Red Sox in the first American League playoff. But this was Feller's twelfth season. His best four years he had given to the U.S. Navy during World War II. He was supposed to pitch in the 1954 World Series, but the Indians lost four straight, and Al Lopez felt that he could not afford to give the old guy his last chance.

Inside the sports store Mr. Feller was sitting at a card table around near the back. There werent any customers around. Everyone was outside catching the free concert. But this was the kid who had come up to the majors at the age of seventeen and struck out seventy-six batters in the sixty-two innings he pitched that first year! Sitting at that card table, he looked about the way he had looked during his last season—hair combed straight back with water, face that looked as if it had never left Van Meter, Iowa.

I walked right up and said hello, or rather not hello but

some other word, as if there werent any formality to be got over. I am not good at talking to famous people. They scare the hell out of me. But then this great pitcher was up here in Victoria, Canada, and what would he think?

I put my hands about nine inches apart.

"Masi was out by this much," I said.

"It was twice that," he replied quickly.

Reading Baseball

EVEN AS A KID YOU KNEW that the baseball movies were terrible. You went to them—*The Pride of the Yankees, The Stratton Story*, et cetera—but in your heart you knew they were terrible. It was not just that William Bendix did not look like Babe Ruth; you knew from all the submarine movies in which Bendix was a dumb but lovable NCO that he was not big enough, not big enough for myth, as you might call it later.

If Jackie Robinson played himself in his movie, you knew he was too old. In most of the movies a team from New York would have the letters *N* and *Y* side by side on their hats. Most of those Hollywood actors couldnt even throw the ball right. Ronald Reagan played a Hall of Fame pitcher in one movie, and they had to shoot it in reverse because he was left-handed and the Hall of Famer was not.

As a kid you knew that the movies stunk because they were made by fat guys with cigars who had been born in Europe and didnt know anything about baseball. A little while ago I saw *Major League III—Back to the Minors*, and it was full of stupid mistakes any ten-year-old could have caught. But there were books. Baseball works very well on radio and it works very well in books.

I grew up in the Interior of British Columbia. I didnt see a major league baseball game till I was thirty-one years old. I saw Europe for the first time when I was thirty. What I am talking about here is fiction. In the Interior of British Columbia I read novels about Europe and I was one of the many thousands of hinterland folk who maintained the collective fiction of major league baseball.

That's what it always was, a collective fiction. Where can one more clearly see the way the bargain of fiction works? What is it that is being settled there on the field inside the building where the automobile does not intrude? How many times has a kid been nonplussed by the fact that his mother couldnt care less that his team just lost the sixth game?

When I was a kid growing up in the Interior of British Columbia there was no television, so Mel Parnell and the guys at Fenway Park were fiction just the way that Perry Mason and Della Street were for my father.

So a kid like that—he read everything he could get hold of, and it was amazing what he could get hold of in that little town in the sticks. He read every word in the papers and collected all the magazines, and still has them in his attic. He read every book there was, and it was, according to the logic above, all fiction.

My Greatest Day in Baseball was as necessary to the imagination as *The Red-Headed Outfield*. The advent of television and adulthood did a lot to change the economy of the imagination. Now I know the difference between an as-told-to biography and a new novel about the grand old game.

Boys' baseball novels were a specific genre in the olden days. Clare Bee and Zane Grey produced plenty of them, aiming the syntax and plot-to-characterization ratio right at the juvenile head. The most prolific of the boys' baseball novelists was the redoubtable Lester Chadwick, who wrote long lists of such books. At the bottoms of the list inside the back cover it always said: "Other volumes in preparation." He penned one series about sports heroes in college, but his greatest success was the long, long series of novels about a wondrous and decent pitcher named Baseball Joe.

"It's a heap of money," agreed Joe, "and I do hate to pass it up. But I won't accept. I'm not an actor and I know it and they know it. I'd simply be capitalizing my popularity. I'd feel like a freak in a dime museum."

Baseball Joe understood the proper relationship between the acting business and the baseball business. If you enjoy sentiments such as his, check out *Baseball Joe in the World Series*, New York, Cupples & Leon, 1917.

But there are certain writers who will, though you encounter them in your normal adolescent pursuits, introduce you to adult versions of your dreams. For me, those writers were Damon Runyan and Ring Lardner. Even in my questionable adulthood, when I wrote a letter to Al Purdy, I said at some point, "You know me, Al."

In 1916, Ring Lardner published his first book of fiction, when he was thirty-one, an epistolary novel or story-sequence entitled *You Know Me, Al; A Busher's Letters*. It was published by Bobbs-Merrill, a company that has always been more than hospitable to writers of serious baseball fiction. *You Know Me, Al* purports to be a series of letters by a rube who rides his great baseball talents into the major leagues.

Ring Lardner, unlike Lester Chadwick, was a great American satirist. Thus it was fortuitous that the young baseball and book fan should fall upon his works, because it is a sense of humour that separates the baseball fan from the football fan or hockey fan. The football fan or hockey fan is the slogan-chanting fellow who throws beer on you if you are sitting in front of him. The baseball fan has time during his three hours in the fresh air (if he is fortunate enough not to live where the anti-baseball developers rule) to look around and see whether there is anything funny going on.

At Jarry Park in Montreal, during the early days of the dismal but adorable Expos, there was a guy who without introduction played a fiddle on the roof of the Expo dugout. In the same section there was a guy who quite often bought a grandstand seat for his duck.

I think that Ring Lardner understood that kind of person. Anyone who has not read *You Know Me, Al* should get his or her hands on it, and its sequel *Treat 'Em Rough: Letters from*

Jack the Kaiser Killer. This one was published in 1918, and you can tell where baseball goes in this instance, over to that other setting for fiction.

But Ring Lardner was a sports journalist. Zane Grey wrote westerns. Neither, then, was quite inside the doors of the house of fiction, at least as it was renovated by Henry James. When I got to university and began to pose as a serious young writer in the UBC cafeteria, I was really taking a chance every time I showed up carrying *The Gas-House Gang* instead of *The Brothers Karamazov*.

Now, of course, baseball books have become chic. Hardly a day goes by that someone, a bookseller, a woman academic, an employee of my wife, does not press a new baseball title on me. The field is so crowded that one no longer regrets leaving some new baseball book on the rack unopened. It has been many years since I bought Lamar Herrin's *The Rio Loja Ringmaster*. It is apparently a very hip novel set in the Mexican baseball league. I may get round to it one of these years, as one says about a Joyce Carol Oates novel.

Serious American writers have for a long time included some baseball scenes in their books. William Carlos Williams, in his great novel *White Mule*, has a late chapter called "Fourth of July Doubleheader," in which his small-business protagonist goes to the Polo Grounds to think about the most important decision of his career while watching a game against the Cardinals. Jack Kerouac's novels are peppered with scenes in which his narrator reads the ball scores in *The Sporting News* or describes his childhood homemade baseball league game.

We all (we baseball virgins) had homemade baseball leagues when we were kids. Kerouac's worked with playing cards. Mine used a handful of dice. The best-known such game appears in Robert Coover's *The Universal Baseball Association, Inc., J. Henry Waugh, Prop.*, one of the first "literary" novels to observe baseball throughout its plot. Coover is one of the most interesting experimental writers in the U.S.A., and his baseball book is a radical questioning of the nature of creation. The league and its happenings (including decisions on which players will die this season) all occur in the mind of Coover's central character, an aging accountant whose name, J. H. Waugh, sounds a lot like Jahweh.

Philip Roth writes in the strong tradition of American satire, and hence had to join his love of baseball to his vocation, the excoriation of American venalities. The result was *The Great American Novel*, a book that was trashed by the American critics who wanted Roth to continue telling the standard stories about growing up Jewish and sensitive in New Jersey. They complained that the novel depended for a lot of its humour on bad taste. That is true, thank goodness.

They also complained that it was too long. I hear the same kind of people saying that baseball games are too long. Roth probably knew that was coming. Good writers who write about baseball do not care what the stuffed shirts who have never been to the bleachers care about their baseball books.

Roth seized upon the American hunger for great traditions, and he knows that the writer of the great American novel would be treated like the next man to bat .400 in the great American game. In *The Great American Novel* he takes advantage of American readiness to identify the myths of baseball and America itself, to poke his twisted satirical blade deep into the pious rah-rah clichés of baseball. In addition he writes a ninety-page account of a ball game against the team from a looney bin, the funniest baseball story I have ever read. One gets the impression that W. P. Kinsella liked it a lot, too.

Mark Harris published a number of adult weepy novels about baseball during this time, and there was the beginning of the current deluge of literate baseball nonfiction, by the likes of Roger Kahn and Roger Angell. All this time one of the most famous baseball novels from the high-rent district was *The Natural*, by Bernard Malamud. People who do not know much about baseball, but who know that I am fond of it, tell me that I must like *The Natural*. Well, I did not like it when the book was new, and I still did not like it when the movie came out, though I must say that Hollywood makes it look more like baseball than they used to.

Here is why I did not like it. It seems to me that Professor Malamud had a look at baseball and decided that it could use some heavy symbolism, to make an epic from its homely details. Everyone by now knows the story—a guy named Roy Hobbes, too old for the game he likes, makes a baseball bat out of a lightning-blasted tree and uses it to have one grand season in the bigs. Well, I felt as if Professor Malamud was a carpetbagger. Baseball does not need myths brought over from the dictionary of mythology.

That gripe over, let me tell you about a baseball novel I love—*The Seventh Babe*, by Jerome Charyn. Charyn, usually described as "zany," has published about a novel a year over the past thirty years. I love him. I love the fact that he is always trying something new—New York cops, the FDR administration, Buffalo Bill, the concentration camps for Japanese-Americans during the war.

The Seventh Babe has a simple premise: Babe Ragland, the seventh player to get that nickname since Ruth's appearance, is a left-handed third baseman who joins the Boston Red Sox in 1923 and starts to fill the ballpark that had emptied after Ruth was traded to the Yankees. Ragland, a kind of updating of Lardner's rube, messes around with a woman who belongs to management and gets blacklisted from the majors. Ragland then lies about his race and becomes a regular with the Cincinnati Colored Giants, a team that travels in a convoy of Buicks and plays in cemeteries and other such parks.

Any fan of baseball (someone with a sense of humour, remember) and reader of hip fiction will love it. Not only is Charyn a daring inventor of plot; he is also a very funny and fast stylist. If our hypothetical literate baseball fan is like me, he will go to Charyn for his baseball book and stay for his table-tennis book, for his Pinocchio book, for his Viet Nam book, et cetera.

The opposite to Charyn's wild inventing ought to be the documentary novel. Have a look at Joel Oppenheimer's *The Wrong Season* some time. Oppenheimer listened to the New Yorkers say that 1972 would be the year that the dismal New York Mets came back to conquer the National League. Oppenheimer decided that the resurgence would be a fine subject for a novel, so he recorded his following of the hopeless louts by radio, TV, and in person.

The book is filled with poems about baseball, portraits of the author/narrator's family, wise words about the conduct of life, and mainly terrific funny/sad writing about observed failure in one's most useless love interests. The book reminded me of Turgenev's hunting stories, though some other fan might see no such connection. I can tell you that you can derive a great deal from the book without caring to remember what the 1972 final standings looked like.

But finally, I have to say that my favourite baseball fictions are written by Fielding Dawson, a contemporary and friend of Oppenheimer. Dawson does not write Baseball Joe stories. In his books about love and art and childhood, baseball is just *there* a lot of the time. For forty years I have not gone through a day without thinking of baseball. Dawson's books are like that.

A Great Day for a Ballgame is about a writer's love affair with an editor. *The Mandalay Dream* is about a man's re-encountering of his childhood. *The Greatest Story Ever Told* is about a boy's teenage sexuality. In each of them, as in Dawson's other books, baseball is just what and where it sensibly should be. It is not a guilty pleasure for an intellectual, and it is not a ritualized event that needs the veneer of myth to make it worthwhile.

A great day for a ball game is a great day for just about anything.

The poets have been writing about baseball indefatigably for years and years, but what the poets do is seldom chic. So there will be lots of baseball books out there. Hell, there will be lots of *Blue Jays* books.

If you have time for just one baseball novel in your busy reading life, you might want to try George Plimpton's *The Curious Case of Sidd Finch*. Plimpton has for a couple decades been the backer of a very important poetry magazine, and it would be hard to deny his interest in sports. *Sidd Finch*, though, was his first sports novel.

In the pages of *Sports Illustrated* in the April 1, 1985 issue, as a matter of fact, there was an article about a phenom named Sidd Finch, a simple country boy who had enormous bare feet, played the French horn, studied Buddhism (hence the two *d*s in his first name), and could throw a baseball accurately at 168 mph. Given that Bob Feller and Nolan Ryan were stopped at about 100 mph, you would have thought that no readers would be sucked in. No one I knew was, of course.

But apparently Plimpton's article—graced with photos that never quite showed the kid's face clearly—did con the gullible. Well, baseball is a democratic game, as they keep telling us. Unlike football and basketball and horseracing, it is played by people who look a little ordinary. It has been played at the major league level by a pitcher who had only three fingers, a pitcher with a wooden leg, an outfielder with a missing arm, chain-smoking first basemen, potbellied pitchers, and diabetic shortstops.

Yet it has always made room for characters who are a little bizarre, who are, as they say, the stuff of fiction. No-Neck Williams, Spaceman Lee, and Larvell Sugar-Bear Blanks all played in the American League in the 1970s. In a number of Walter Mitty books, George Plimpton tried to make himself a character out of the book world who could step into the shoes (and shoulder pads) of the "real" sports universe. With his bird, Sidd Finch, he finally got the relationship between fiction and baseball right.

In all my prolixity I have written only one baseball story, though I have committed a few poems along the way. I have never given in to the temptation to start a baseball novel. But I do like to slip a baseball scene or at least a reference into all my fictions. When I was writing my novel *Caprice* I thought that I would forget about baseball for once. The book was set, after all, in the rangeland of B.C. around 1889. Then, while I was doing research I read that a baseball game in Kamloops was delayed in the fifth inning on New Year's Day that year because of an eclipse of the sun. What could I do?

Taking the Field

HAVE YOU EVER HEARD hockey fans and basketball fans and auto-racing fans complain that, as a game, baseball is too slow? You bet. But have you ever heard a *writer* complain that baseball is too slow? Not a chance. I once heard a hockey reporter say it, but he isnt really a writer. I mean a *writer*.

A large proportion of the writers I know play some sort of baseball, usually softball. Not that stupid desecration called slo-pitch. Maybe medium-pitch. Maybe medium-fast. They carry their personal stats in their heads, and they get a new piece of equipment every season—a batting glove this year, say.

Baseball *is* slow, sometimes. It is slow when it should be, and suddenly very fast when it should be. It is like thinking and writing. If you are a writer, you will recognize and value both the slow and the fast. How long did it take you to write that story? someone will ask, and you will say all your life. But remember how the quick sentences slid out and settled into place.

Remember how still Carl Yastrzemski stood at the plate while the pitcher fooled around, and then how swiftly that bat came around, and how slowly he was allowed to run around the bases because the ball was arcing high into the right-field stands.

It is not absolutely necessarily true that writers like baseball. For all I know, Emily Dickinson didnt like baseball. It is not even necessarily true that male writers like baseball. But if you look around the ball yards and the bookstores, you will see that male writers have more to say about baseball than they do about other sports. Boxing is probably in second place. It appeals to battlers such as Norman Mailer and Joyce Carol Oates.

Over the past few years there have been lots of explanations offered for the connection between writing and the diamond—explanations earnest, fanciful, and semiotic. There's your childhood in the gloaming, decades ago in the stubble grass of South Saskatchewan. There's Tim Raines stepping into the batter's box, top of the first, and wiping out the rear chalk line someone has just drawn a moment before. There's that definable odour of fried onions coming from the hot dog in the hand of the kid in front of you. I haven't hit on anything exactly right yet, have I?

One warm February day in Puerto Limon, Costa Rica, 1978, I wandered into old concrete Big Boy Stadium, and found myself a wooden seat up behind home plate. There was an old black guy hitting fungos to four skinny young black guys in centre field. I figured it must be a kind of pre season rookie camp. Here's what's funny: I was not surprised to recognize the old guy hitting the fungos, as well as the other old guy loafing on a seat right behind the chicken wire. I remembered them from the ballpark in Oliver, B.C., Canada, where I sold Orange Crush and retrieved foul balls for dimes, and later climbed up on the roof to take over my dad's job as official scorer.

There I was, sitting over a ball game, pen in hand.

Now a lot of grown-up fellows sit over a page, a ball game in their heads.

Baseball is a funny game. You've heard that. It can be unfunny, too. Ask Red Sox fans about Bill Buckner's grounder. Sometimes baseball can resemble the stupidity and hurt of your life. Sometimes it is 8–0 in the fifth inning, and it's just a June game between San Diego and Atlanta, and you wonder why you're not upstairs groating the bathtub.

But look. In baseball we dont talk about the long bomb and the safety blitz and sudden death. What do we want to do in the ball game? We want to get home. We have the only big-deal game I know in which the ball is put into play by the defence. Unlike football, soccer, hockey, and basketball, our game is not ruled by lines in space or ticks in time. It is not existential. It is a dream come true. If the dream perishes (check out those Red Sox fans), there's another game tomorrow. If it is October, there is spring training after a few months of early darkness and Cavs' games.

Remember when the sixty-five-year-old painter David Siqueiros was sprung from prison so that he could finish the murals in Maximilian's palace in Mexico City in time for the World Cup tournament, the government wanted to release him at noon. There was a big crowd of supporters waiting to take him away in triumph. But Siqueiros played first base for a ball team inside the walls, and he made the people outside cool their heels till the afternoon's game was over.

Playing the game is the best experience, even if you are sixty. Sitting in the grandstand in Edmonton is an activity (yes, activity) to be cherished. Reading baseball fiction is a very good thing to do, during season or off-season.

Homers vs. Poetry

HE TRUE BASEBALL FAN is a terrible snob. It would be pretty hard to be a snob about hockey or football—and that is just another opinion of a true baseball snob.

Major League Baseball added two new teams again in 1998. When baseball goes through an expansion year, and that was an expansion year if there ever was one, the baseball snob gets snobbier. Baseball snobs hate expansion. And whenever there is an expansion year there are a lot of home runs in baseball. Baseball snobs dont like home-run circuses.

All that year we kept hearing that the home-run race, led by Mark McGwire, Sammy Sosa, and Ken Griffey, was just what baseball needed to bounce back from the disaffection caused by the great strike of a couple years earlier. More and more people were getting interested in baseball because it looked as if those three men had a chance of beating Roger Maris's record of sixty-one home runs.

The baseball snob doesnt care about all these new fans. They are the same kind of people who dont start following the baseball season until the World Series. These are the people who bring cellphones to the ballpark. The true baseball snob cant wait until these people forget baseball and go back to watching some mindless car race or the Spice Girls, or whoever the tuneless singing stars are this year.

Because baseball is a game of the mind, right? The real baseball fan sits in the bleachers while there is a slight rain dampening the empty benches all around him, and wonders whether the manager will have the nerve to call for a sacrifice bunt attempt on a two-strike pitch with the third baseman playing back. He sneers when the less recondite applaud an easy catch in left field.

I am a baseball snob. Have been since I was ten years old.

I can tell you who Roger Maris hit his sixty-first home run off. So I did not get carried away by McGwire, Sosa, and Griffey, right? Well, maybe McGwire, because I had him on my fantasy team, and I was in first place. Okay, Sammy Sosa, because he's not an American, and we not-Americans cheer for each other. Oh, what the hay, I liked it when Junior hit one, too, because he played for Seattle, and Seattle is sort of Vancouver.

All right, all right. I was hoping they would all do it. I hoped McGwire would win the race, but I wanted them all to hit more than sixty. It was a heck of a rush when that huge redhead put a dent in the scoreboard. Sammy! He reaches for a pitch a foot outside the strike zone, and hits one out to tie the game in the ninth, every damned time. And Ken Griffey? Ah, the heck with him. He wears his baseball hat backward. I hate that.

A lot of amazing things happened that year. A fat guy with a sloppy shirt pitched a perfect game. A muffin-faced rookie came up and set strikeout records before he was old enough to vote. He missed the whole next year because of a dead arm. A shortstop that was twenty-one got forty homers and forty stolen bases. A shortstop! The New York Yankees set a new record for games won in a season. All us baseball snobs hate the New York Yankees.

When Mark McGwire looked as if he was ready to rap his sixty-second dinger with that beautiful automatic one-hand swing of his, CBC television had me in a seat in front of the giant TV screen at a sports bar across the street in back of their building. The Cardinals' game was on, of course, and the sports bar had antennae all over their roof, just like the CBC building across the street. The technical guys were getting frantic because some police standoff with an armed man was going on a few blocks away and all the good equipment was gone. They patched me up with microphones and cellphones and pagers and wires inside all my clothes. The idea was that McGwire would smack a home run while the suppertime TV news was on, and they would cut to the bar, where I would make my on-the-spot commentary.

If he hit it in the first inning, it would be too early for the news, and the equipment wasnt working yet anyway. If he waited till his last at-bat, the news would be over, and CBC would be showing some drama about young idiots in New York apartments. Well, it was that kind of year. In the middle of the news, McGwire hit a very un-McGwirish homer, a line drive just over the fence at the left-field foul pole, and the bright lights were on me. It was as noisy as all get-out in that bar, and I had consumed a few careful pints, but I did my sports-remarking really well, and remembered that when I was a high school kid, this is what I wanted to grow up to be.

So I might be a baseball snob, but in 1998 my fantasy team set a record for home runs, and in the real world the home-run record was in the National League for a welcome change. Besides, any time the home-run guys can take the spotlight away from the New York Yankees, I say hooray for the long ball! Go yard! Hit it out of here! Touch them all! Goodbye, baseball!

THE SIXTIES

What I Saw and Heard in the Sixties

I N 1971 I WAS playing shortstop for the Granville Grange Zephyrs in Vancouver's illustrious Kosmik League, and we had a catcher by the name of Brian "Cat" Fisher. Several games into the season we were sitting side by side on the ground we called a "dugout." He was putting on his catcher duds and I was probably rubbing in some pain reliever.

"Sure are a lot of people named Brian Fisher," I said. "There's a famous Canadian painter named Brian Fisher."

"I'm him," said the catcher.

That's a meaningless exchange. But somehow, for me, it marks the moment when I turned thirty-five. After that I would buy a house, as the banks put it, and start getting Brian Fisher paintings to hang on the walls.

I have been in love with art and needed it for my poems at least since the moment I saw an original Rufino Tamayo in 1958. I bought a Van Gogh flowers-in-a-jug picture reproduced on canvas from a guy who got it at the Pacific National Exhibition in 1959. In the sixties I started buying art. I mean drawings and paintings you could hang on the wall. I also got some art given to me by my painter friends. I thank them for that, and I know that the books I gave them in return weren't much of a return.

Now my house is full of paintings and prints and constructions and so on by Brian Fisher, Roy Kiyooka, Charlie Pachter, and Greg Curnoe. I also have a couple of Matisses, three Cuevases, a Riopelle, a Dennis Burton, two Kenneth Patchens, and so on. Not much art by women. I'd like to get an object made by Gathy Falk or a big prairie landscape by Dorothy Knowles.

In the nineteen sixties, people got serious about pop culture and treated it for its political-social implications. Treated it as art. The popular image of visual art was the psychedelic San Francisco rock-and-roll poster with its nearly unreadable list of bands that were going to appear at the Fillmore. The popular image of musical art was the Grateful Dead singing about drugs and love, and running extravagant riffs way down the handle of the guitar. The popular image of clothing was something like the popular image of visual art wrapped around the players who made the popular image of musical art.

In the very early sixties, before the incense and beads culture began, I went to San Francisco and sometimes even the Haight-Ashbury. I didnt go back there till the late seventies. I missed all that time during which undereducated teenagers from Illinois padded barefoot up to you on Haight Street and asked whether you had any spare U.S. currency. But I knew it was going on. I went to the first love-in at Stanley Park and bought the first demo-forty-five by Country Joe and the Fish. I carried Grace Slick's first album to Detroit and played it for the ears at the People's Workshop there.

But psychedelic posters and raga-rock albums were not my meat and potatoes, not even my tofu and sprouts.

An aside: people often trash the fifties for being square and smug, for being Pat Boone and Dwight Eisenhower. But I remember the fifties as Marlon Brando and Jack Kerouac and James Dean and Charlie Parker.

So the sixties. People mention the Beatles and Pop Art and dashikis at Southern lunch counters and magic mushrooms, et cetera, the white kids' decade. When the counter culture was sold across the counter.

In the sixties I was given the music of Albert and Don Ayler, and it was given to me by a Canadian painter and a U.S. American poet who lived a hundred and fifty miles apart and didnt know each other.

The American poet was John Sinclair. In 1966 he and some other somewhat disaffected U.S.A. people lived a couple blocks from the desolate Northbound Freeway in Detroit, in a whole block rescued from urban blight, as they say. Poets, musicians, druggies, anarchists, disobeyers of the U.S. rules about racial separation, lived in the various apartments, and on the outside, up high, in foot-high letters, were the words: COME ON PEOPLE NOW SMILE ON YOUR BROTHER EVERYBODY GET TOGETHER TRY TO LOVE ONE ANOTHER RIGHT NOW. In those days brothers included sisters.

John Sinclair's group, the Artists' Workshop, had a couple years earlier got a mailing list from our Vancouver magazine, *Tish*, which a few years earlier had got a mailing list from Diane DiPrima's New York magazine, *The Floating Bear*. In the sixties the writing groups gave each other things. John edited a mimeo poetry magazine called *Work* and a mimeo music magazine called *Change*. The music he was interested in was made by black people, jazz and blues and the strange stuff arising then called various things, free music, usually. Made by Sun Ra and Archie Shepp, Giuseppe Logan, and Noah Howard.

In the forties, when I was eight years old, I was a fan of both Benny Goodman and Prez, and in those days American radio stations played that stuff, before they discovered that you could make more money playing children's music. In the fifties I collected jazz, again black and white, on forty-fives, and later I went to sleep in the air force with Shorty Rogers in my ear. In the sixties I wrote a few poems to and about the jazz I knew—Stan Getz meets Jerry Mulligan, I think.

Then I moved to Calgary. There wasnt any jazz in Calgary. There wasnt any radio-station jazz because the cows didnt like giving milk to that weird Afric bebop in the barn. No record stores. No art either. Soon as I got to Calgary, 1963, I asked where's the art gallery. I was directed to a framing shop on South Seventeenth Avenue that also had some landscapes in the window, selling for a hundred and fifty bucks. Well, Calgary. Now that I am moved east and west, Calgary has a terrific art gallery. Call it a museum.

So I had got a little stuck. I didnt have a record player in Calgary—what was the point? Once in Oliver I heard my favourite DJ, Bowen at KSL, introducing Ornette Coleman, and I fell down on the kitchen lino, I mean this alto guy wasnt much older than I, and he was a science fiction genius of the Texas black intellect gone somewhere you couldnt go but wished to hell you could, go.

But by the time I got to London, Ontario, 1966, I was fresh from a first tour of Europe, got kicked out of the Vienna Folks' Opera for no jacket, only cardigan and tie. Greg Curnoe had a lot of great albums in his studio, but John Sinclair lived in Detroit, after all, you knew that paradigm skyscraper skyline. And Sinclair, well, like a lot of U.S.A. young poets in those days, must have come from a rich family, had that kind of ease—he could just walk in the back door of a blues club and do an interview with Jimmy Reed. Boy, it was neat to be a young poet on the way and Hanging Around in Deetroit, listen to stuff you knew had to be made by something that Mattered, black bodies under the steel wheels of America gone too far.

I just fell flat. I dont know whether you are familiar with the music I am talking about. Most of it was made on Delmark Records from Chicago and ESP records from New York. It was screeching and honking of saxes, drums that did not KEEP time, no, but made melody under the delightful noise. No time register. No notes, said Albert Ayler. The professional bigger business labels let a little seep up to them, John Coltrane eventually on those lovely packaged ABC Impulse! records, say, soon to be followed by Shepp and Pharaoh Sanders.

John Coltrane died at age thirty-nine, Albert Ayler

made it to thirty-five. I always thought those numbers meant something.

If you would like to hear my favourite album from the sixties, listen to ESP 10059. That's "Eastern Man Alone" by the Charles Tyler Ensemble—Tyler's alto saxophone along with a cello and two basses.

I didnt like what happened to John Sinclair and his music in 1967. A year earlier he had steel shelves of jazz and blues albums reached right up to the ceiling, had them tidy and delightful, kept his stylus clean. But some time in the beginning of 1967, U.S.A. politics became such that drugs for recreation were too easily available. I mean if there is a bag of it just lying there on the windowsill, well, USE it.

So here is the scene in the middle of 1967: there is stuff lying all over the place, including teenagers from small prairie towns, and there isnt much jazz. Now rock-and-roll records lie all over the place, Sinclair grabs a gummy stack of them and jams them onto his machine. Swoosh go lips with boo cigs in them, and the room is full of noise.

Well, I have to give him credit. He was stoned all the time. His hair was three feet wide. But he had this old-timy jazz-ear sentiment about rock: the musicians ought to be able to play their instruments. He liked a Detroit band called the Northbound Freeway, and he became the manager of a very successful Detroit band called the MC5.

But he became famous. I was pulled off a Greyhound at Windsor because I said I was going to be reading poems for a gig managed by John Sinclair. Eventually, after Sinclair stepped over from music politics to the kind of politics that scare the U.S. police, he was set up by a narc agent. Everyone knew this dip was a narc, but when he whined and begged for a joint, John finally gave him one. This resulted in John's going to the slam, and becoming the white panther.

The narc had one of those unbelievably silly names that crop up in U.S. news banality. I always get his name mixed up with the name of the guy who was driving the vehicle that James Dean's Spyder hit. One of them was named Donald Turnipseed. The other was Warner Stringfellow.

The Canadian painter was Greg Curnoe. In the late sixties, London Ontario, as they say, was the hottest artist town in the nation, and Curnoe was the hottest artist in town. But if you said that he would snuff the back of his hand across his moustache and say something that means "aw shucks." Country Greg, I once heard Michael Snow call him. My wife and I called him that from then on.

Curnoe helped me find out about free jazz, too. He was then making lots of anti-U.S.A. remarks and art, such as his famous map of North America in which there is no U.S.A. between Canada and Mexico, but he loved American music, especially Black American music. So I heard a lot of Albert Ayler and Sunny Murray in Greg's studio.

I also heard his assault force, the Nihilist Spasm Band, every week at the York Hotel pub. Look out the open door and watch old-time railroad guys with a few dollars in their pockets, look inside and decide to keep on walking. The Nihilist Spasm Band played with homemade and ridiculous instruments and made a great amount of noise and played what might be described as eight different and simultaneous rhythms at all times, except during the 2.5-string bass solos from Hugh McIntyre. Once they let me sit in on drums, but soon pulled me off the chair for keeping time. (In the mid-nineties I stood in on electric guitar with the amplified NSB in Port Colborne. I was deaf for four days, as bandmember Dr. John Clement had told me I would be.)

While we were living in London Ontario, Angela and I went over to the Curnoes' place many nights, because they had a baby to tuck in and we didnt. We sat up till four in the morning, us young people, talking about art and Europe and Canadian politics and the book trade, just about the time that Canadians were getting wound up for Centennial. Sat up on kitchen chairs painted bright red and blue and yellow, Curnoe colours. He won the Centennial Cake Decoration contest that year, a huge cake with orange and blue Canadian-bacon-flavoured icing, and he wore a yellow suit with black buttons to the ceremony in Ottawa. A real influence on me: for the next four years I wore bright green or yellow or red trousers on the streets of Montreal.

In Vancouver, just as I was starting off, I had lived among poets and painters, and thought that this was the pattern of my life. But then I had three lonely years in Calgary, teaching English to fundamentalist teenagers and paying off school loans. Now we were in London Ontario, surrounded by painters who were sometimes musicians and occasionally writers. Looked good. I learned a great deal that year, and now, in retrospect, that eleven months in London Ontario seems as long as my four years in Montreal.

The art magazines and even the rotogravures were paying a lot of attention to the London art scene that year. My diary is filled with colour pictures of my friends' works. The genius Jack Chambers was back from Spain, making incomprehensible movies with multiple sound systems. Tony Urquhart was somewhere, probably at the university, where N. E. Baxter Thing had been artist in residence the previous semester. The younger painters and sculptors and airplane makers could be found at the York or at Curnoe's studio or at the 20/20 Gallery, where Greg and I started the Beaver Kosmos occurrences. I cant without awkwardness name them all, but Ron Martin was there, John Boyle and the Rabinovitch brothers and Murray Favro.

Greg didnt like having Ron Martin come around to his studio. In one of Greg's huge block-letter paintings you will see an outsize spelling mistake and an annotation to the effect that Martin had just tromped up the stairs.

The country was coming together. Its strands were

making some kind of order. Or at least around me I saw connections being made, which is amazing, given the fact that it takes a week to drive across the country. Greg Curnoe didnt know Roy Kiyooka, but I found out that they both liked Stanley Spencer a lot. So I gave Greg Roy's book of poems about Stanley Spencer, and the next year in Montreal I introduced these two painters to one another. Their paintings address one another still across the hall upstairs at my house.

But mainly I was learning, thirty years old and wide-eyed, I mean I knew about the minor poems of Philip Lamantia, let us say, but there was Greg, 3:30 A.M., telling me about Dada, rubbing his knuckles on his hairy scalp, telling me why he could think in the same minute about Hugo Ball and a kid artist in Beale Tech High School named Chris Dewdney.

I left London Ontario after a year because I was offered the job of writer in residence at Sir George Williams University in Montreal. I asked my wife Angela, would she rather live next year in London Ontario or Montreal, and she voted for Montreal. It was the year of Canada's centenary, and so there was a world's fair in Montreal. That would make it a little tough to get an apartment. There were two apartments for rent in the western half of Montreal in August 1967. One was over a Greek cafe on Greene Street. We took the other one. It had a lot of walls to hang images on.

When I was a Ph.D. student in London Ontario, I told myself that I would like to work or rather teach at either Sir George Williams University or Simon Fraser University, or both of them. They were both new and too new to have settled down.

Montreal and music; Montreal and art. I felt pretty lucky because there was a *boîte* called the Barrel, where the ESP musicians played. I went my first week in Montreal to hear and see (!) Albert Ayler, with Don Ayler and Rashied Ali and I cant remember who the bass player was, probably Henry

Grimes. I went alone, as I have gone to most things in my life, and sat up close, couldnt afford more than one beer. Rashied Ali fluttered his drum sticks so fast that one flew from his hand and I caught it on the first bounce and handed it back to him. I once went to a hockey game with my father. He caught a puck that flew into the crowd, and he tossed it back on the ice. I liked him for that.

Two weeks later the Barrel closed. Music was slim pickings after that. Three years later I heard Paul Bley and Barry Altschul at the university. They played to an audience of about ten. I didnt know anyone in Montreal who liked free jazz.

But Roy Kiyooka taught art at Sir George Williams University. The sixties were becoming a circle. In the very early sixties I knew Kiyooka as a guru poet-painter in Vancouver. In the middle sixties I knew his brother, Harry Kiyooka, who taught painting at the University of Calgary. Roy didnt know anything about Albert Ayler, but he was a very hip person. In fact, in those years we were living similar lives, except that he had three daughters. We just assumed that it was the natural order of things to get university jobs around the country. He was in Montreal now, but he had recently been teaching in Halifax. Later we would both go back to Vancouver and more or less stay there, except for temporary gigs elsewhere, he in Kyoto, for example, I in Berlin.

In other ways I have always thought that Greg Curnoe and I had parallel careers. But he was famous for sticking at home in London Ontario. Country Greg.

In 1965, when my second book of poems was published in Mexico, it contained a dozen of Kiyooka's photo collages in ellipsoid shape. This would become the shape of all his art for a decade—paintings, sculpture, books.

In 1967, when I got to Montreal, Kiyooka was associated with a group of hard-edge painters at the Galérie du Siècle, with Molinari and Hurtubise and Toussignant, the hottest painters on the so-called island in those days. Molinari was doing vertical stripes. Toussignant was doing gongs that jiggled your optic nerve. Hurtubise was doing little bent shapes. Kiyooka was doing ellipses. These guys were making large paintings with acrylics, using tape and X-Acto knives.

When they had a *galérie* show in English Canada, Greg Curnoe was commissioned to make a poster for it. He did it with coloured printed letters of the painters' names, and running around the edge, the name Gallery of the Century. I loved the effrontery and the wit.

In my one year in London Ontario, and my four years in Montreal, I learned a great deal about music and painting, and I kept on writing, as was my habit. But in those years my writing was, to me, the least interesting writing of my life.

Though in 1969 I won the Governor General's Award in English poetry, the promotion committee of the Department of English at Sir George Williams University refused to give me a raise because as far as they knew I didnt publish. They didnt know anything about Albert Ayler or Greg Curnoe, either.

But in 1967 Curnoe was in Montreal. Around centennial year the airports in Canada were being decorated with paintings by Canadian artists. In an example of their per-spicacity the thinkers at the Department of Transport decided not to show anything like local art. So Brian Fisher and Ron Bloore from Saskatchewan had paintings at Dorval airport. Molinari had a painting at Vancouver International. Greg Curnoe was putting up a mural in the underground international-flights walkway at Dorval.

Bob Fones, the young London Ontario artist, and I were helping. And it was hard work. The wall of the underground walkway was made of Italian marble, very hard stone, as hard as the heart of the mayor of Montreal, who made flim-sier walls to hide the poverty slums of Montreal from the eyes of tourists. Greg bought dozens of hard drill bits and we broke our wrists trying to make holes in the marble.

But after a week or so the mural was up, several panels detailing the history of flight and other stuff in Canada. It incorporated an airplane propeller that operated and led the authorities to insist that a cage be built around it. There were a lot of authorities coming down to the international-flights underground walkway.

Unfortunately, "international" meant largely U.S. American, and during this Expo summer there were a lot of U.S. Americans visiting the city of Montreal. Unfortunate, because one of the aeronautical figures in Curnoe's huge mural was a representation of a man being decapitated by an airplane propeller. I forget his name, Ernie something, maybe, but Greg averred that he was a figure from south-western Ontario history, even though, as many visitors averred, he bore a likeness, in the painting, to Lyndon B. Johnson, the U.S. president who was disliked in many foreign airports because of his habit of ordering bombing raids over small countries.

The upshot of the affair was that U.S. American tourists were more important than Canadian art, as usual in this country, and employees of the Department of Transport undid all our wrist-breaking work on that marble, and removed the mural. I hear that it has been ever since in either the basement of the Department of Transport building or the basement of the National Gallery. Those are our two main patrons of the visual arts.

When I look around in books that describe the relationships between writers and painters I see that they often do portraits of each other. Everyone knows Pablo Picasso's portrait of Gertrude Stein, but fewer people know Gertrude Stein's portrait of Pablo Picasso. Often the writers do fictional portraits of the painters, but then what else can you do?

I have always been fond of Joe Plaskett's portrait of Phyllis Webb. It should be in the National Gallery or the National Library. There is someone else's portrait of Phyllis Webb in the National Library, but it is not as good as Plaskett's.

Greg Curnoe did some drawings of Canadian writers. I once published his drawing of Victor Coleman on the cover of *Imago*, the poetry magazine I started in the sixties. He also drew David McFadden for a big-little book they made together, and Milton Acorn for the cover of one of his books. Curnoe did a drawing of me once, and it appeared in the catalogue of a drawing show mounted in Halifax, I think. Out of the blue, Sheila Curnoe sent the original to me in 1995, what a darling. It's not bad, but I dont think he got the nose right.

Over the years I have had quite a few portraits done, as I guess anyone who hangs around artists will. Some were by amateurs or poets who can also draw, such as a wonderful drawing by Artie Gold, which I must get framed one of these years. Christian Nicholson, an Ottawa realist painter, did a nice painting of Mavis Gallant and a nice painting of me, though people in the future might be deluded into thinking that I was that good-looking. Roy Kiyooka has done my portrait in a series of photographs, and Peter Whalley did an atrocious caricature. One nice day in Jutland, 1995, Heather Spears did a drawing of me, that sweetie.

The first painting I can remember is really and secretly a collage, and a cooperative work of painter and poet. It was painted by Vancouver artist Gordon Payne in 1962 or 1963: big angry-poet face with dark glasses and what I would look like years later. But if you get close to the picture, you can see that the letters of my first name have been cut from a magazine and affixed to the then-wet paint above my head. A ransom note to the future, I figured.

But no matter how close you get to the picture it is unlikely that you will see the one-page manuscript poem under the paint. Oh, I love things like that! Over the years I have often met people who never took the dustjacket off the hardback edition of my 1971 book *Geneve*, and unfolded it to see what was there. The dedication in *The Gangs of Kosmos* is to the "three people on the cover." If anyone thinks about that, she probably looks at the reproduction of Charlie Pachter's big print called *Champêtre*, notices the figure of the two women (Margaret Atwood and Angela Bowering) in a field edged by trees, and figures that of course the artist is the third person. But if one looks at the centre of the picture, at the trees that appear in the distance, though between the two women, one will see a human figure crucified on a tree. This, said Charlie, is the artist. On the cover of the book the crucified artist appears on the spine.

I have collaborated often with visual artists. I have also envied them their ability to work while listening to the CBC or to Albert Ayler, let us say. When I was a kid, before I knew I would be a writer, I was trying to learn to draw. I thought of being a cartoonist. I sold sixteen giant cartoons for two dollars when I was thirteen years old, and would not get paid for a poem till I was twenty-one.

I have also collaborated with musicians, of course. I was in the high school choir and band, and for a while in first-year college I butchered the drums in a little trio. Back in high school I wrote the lyrics of a lot of songs whose music was written by my lifetime pal Will Trump. He was also part of a singing quartet called the Troubadours, and they performed our songs along with those of Johnny Mercer. At UBC, in the sixties, Will Trump and I wrote a musical set in Japan at the end of the Tokugawa period, but it was performed only at parties and in our Asian studies class.

In the seventies and eighties I provided lyrics for a rock band called Gary Kramer and the Works, and for some less popular or more serious composers, such as John Oliver. It is a neat feeling to see people dancing to your poems, and just as neat to see others sitting quietly in a concert hall and trying to follow your simple tropes. But right now I cant remember collaborating with any musicians in the sixties. I probably did. But there are things one did in the sixties that one cannot recall today.

When it gets to be the nineties and then the nothings everywhere but in your own consciousness, and when you yourself get to be in your sixties, the age of power and maturity, your house gets to be filled with detritus of the earlier decades. The more recent decades have not really gelled yet, but the earlier ones are piled up with weight in little-used rooms. I have hundreds of baseball and sports magazines from the forties and fifties. I have a good record collection from the sixties. I seldom go and riffle the April 1955 issue of *Baseball Digest*, but just a few days ago I was making a tape of a 1965 ESP disc by Charles Tyler. My walls, of course, reflect the gaze of 1967.

For the U.S. Americans, the chief memory will be of the war against Vietnam and the other Indochinese countries. It is embedded in the artworks we have from the decade. Archie Shepp's lovely angry-sounding tenor sax snarls behind the reciting voice of Amiri Baraka (LeRoi Jones) are for me a lot more redolent of Viet Sixties than the preteener psychedelics of Jim Morrison and the Doors. And I never told this to my friend Greg Curnoe, but I do think he must have noticed how much that Ernie guy looked like Lyndon B. Johnson.

ℐMPERSONATING A
WRITER

The Reader and You

WHEN WE WERE SITTING in our rows in high school English class, we were instructed that we should be careful to distinguish between the person who had written the fiction we were reading (usually Katherine Mansfield) and the narrator of that fiction. We were given to understand that this was a matter of the first necessary sophistication, and that from then on we could curl our lip and raise an eyebrow whenever we heard someone say, "Katherine Mansfield said in her story...."

It has taken me more years than I spent in high school to figure out that the principle involved works in other places as well. Here are two such examples:

1. The distinction between the person who writes a poem, even a short tidy lyric poem, and the voice you hear reciting it while you look at the silent book. That is to say, if you tell me that you are reading Whitman, I know that you are listening to the speaker he made up. People are going to tell me that I am discussing the *persona* here. But there is a difference between Prufrock and the voice speaking in a David Bromige poem. Maybe Eliot has two voices between himself and the reader. Anyway, when Whitman wrote that his reader was encountering a man rather than a book, he was protesting against the fate that he knew faced any writer of the first-person singular or "ensemble," that as soon as he writes those words on a piece of paper he has an other to read.

2. The distinction between "the reader" and the person who is holding the silent book and reading it. Sometimes I go so far as to say that the "author" and the "reader" are characters in any story. (The implications are interesting if you extend this structure to speeding tickets and marriage certificates.)

How often have you or I read something in criticism or theory about "the reader" and realized that this construct is as distinct from us as is Patrick Henry or Spider Robinson.

Anyone knows that literature is an idea but reading is what you do. Literature cant hurt you but reading can.

(I am of course in my own ant trap here, because no matter what I do, the "you" I am talking about is not the person reading these words, are you?)

So that construct that certain critics like to write about, "the reader," cant do anything about what is written. But if you are reading a book, you can intervene. You can invent a reading.

You can always skip page thirty-five. You can read from the last page to the first. You can stick pages from a pornographic novel between Northrop Frye's sheets. You can call the narrator of Atwood's second novel Agnes. Or you can intervene simply by reading the way you read.

The person who wrote the book cant stop you. The "author" cant, either. And the "reader" doesnt know you exist.

A lot of what they call "reflexive" writing is simply the result of the writer's trying to be you. You are the ground of the so-called postmodern. Our high school English teachers really knew all this, but they didnt think that it was the kind of thing they were supposed to be teaching us. We knew it, too, but we didnt think we were supposed to think about such things during the high school English game.

Glowing Hearts

ALL MY LIFE I HAVE had trouble with the national anthem. When I was in grade one I had trouble understanding the words to the Lord's Prayer and the words to the national anthem. For instance, "true paytrick love." I figured "paytrick" must be the way they said Patrick back east.

Christmas carols often bothered me, too, of course. "Round yon virgin" had me wondering, until I figured out that a virgin was a sort of stall in a barn. You just went round yon virgin, and there they were: mother and child!

Of course the other true thing in "O Canada" was always a bother, and I think that it still is for people who stop even momentarily to reflect. That is to say, did anyone ever dispute Canada's claim to be the true north? For that matter, what kind of north would a false north be? I can see an argument at the other end of America. Chile and Argentina might start another war about which one is the true south.

When I was a kid there was a dispute about the national anthem. I wanted "Oh Canada," but all the stiff-necked Brits and their toadies in my town insisted that "God Save the King" was the national anthem. It was an argument that was waged across the country, I was given to understand. At ball games and movies and school assemblies the audience was supposed to sing "O Canada" at the start of things and "God Save the King" at the end. I used to sing "God save the foreign monarch," hoping that it was just noticed by the people closest to me.

When I was a kid I couldnt understand why we stood up and sang the national anthem before a baseball game. I still dont understand it. In Canada, we generally have to listen to two anthems, the one about bombs and rockets and "O Canada." I usually slouch and read or eat during the first one, and just kind of stand there for the second. Very few people sing, despite the encouragement from the public address announcer. I have been to baseball, football, and hockey games all over Canada, and the only place I have heard the crowd actually sing the national anthem good and loud was Montreal. Maybe the people singing the English words were trying to drown out the people singing the French words.

Historically, the French words came first. They were written by a person named Adolphe-Basile Routhier, and set to the music of Calixa Lavallée, to be first sung at an ice rink in Québec City in 1880. As one might expect, the English version was written by a Toronto schoolteacher with the true Ontario name of Robert Stanley Weir.

His words have been changed a little in recent years, probably by a relative of a civil servant. When I was a kid, the main feature of the words was loud repetition. Lots of standing on guard and lots of "O Canada"-ing. Now that repetition has been replaced by stupidity.

But I am getting a little ahead of myself. I said that all my life I have had trouble with the national anthem. I would not sing "God Save the King" because I did not want to be a colonial. Now I do not sing "O Canada" because I am not certain that its words apply to me.

Maybe I should go through the poem as we have it now, and state my reservations.

It begins with an exclusion: "O Canada! Our home and native land!" Presumably any Canadian born outside the country stops singing here. I am reminded that a few years ago the literary chauvinists invented a term, "birthright Canadian," to exclude all the U.S.-born writers who were cluttering up the Canadian writing scene.

All right, the immigrants are not eligible to sing our national anthem. The second line continues the work: "True patriot love in all thy sons command." Now all female residents of the true north are supposed to quit singing. I guess Canada's daughters cannot be expected to offer patriot love.

Come to think of it, remember when the young Shelley

got kicked out of university for suggesting that Christianity was based on an unlikely premise? Christianity said that if you choose to have the requisite belief, you will be saved. Shelley pointed out that one cannot make a decision to have a belief. Similarly I would suggest that a country cannot *command* its male offspring to love it.

"With glowing hearts we see thee rise," eh? If we were to be nitpicking, we might say that one sees better with eyes than with hearts, whether they are glowing or not. (How many times have you wanted to sing something that rimes with glowing hearts"?) Even if we are not nitpicking, we might ask about that rising. Where is Canada rising? Is it because of this visible rising that we know our exclusionary country to be the (capitalized) True North?

Well, maybe those women and girls and immigrants are lucky that they dont have to worry about the North, whether it is True in the carpenter's sense or the philosopher's sense. Maybe they also dont have to concern themselves with the logic and grammar of the poem's next line, one of the recent revisions: "From far and wide, O Canada, we stand on guard for thee."

Let us for a moment set aside the problem of how native-born citizens can be from far and wide. Perhaps they have to come from Yukon and Cape Breton to Ottawa in order to sing this song.

Let us look at the sentence. I find it harder to understand than I ever did "paytrick love." How can the singers stand from far and wide? From far and wide we stand? That is simply impossible. People can arrive from far and wide, perhaps, or shout from far and wide. But people cannot stand from anything. My character Bernie in *Fiddler's Night* makes a big point of this impossibility disguised as self-description.

In the sixth line the Canadian-born male singers enjoin the Deity: "God keep our land glorious and free!" At least the Christian and Jewish ones do. All non-believers are here invited out. But what about religious people of another belief? Chances are that most of them were born outside the country, true enough. But what about boys who were born here? Can they substitute Allah or Buddha or L. Ron Hubbard here?

Finally, the small straggling group of native-born God-fearing males sings twice: "O Canada, we stand on guard for thee!" Against whom is this minority group standing guard? Perhaps against the True West and True East. Perhaps against all these females and immigrants and Voodoo adherents who have filled up the country.

If you happen to be one of those people who was dropped from the singing group partway through the song, listen to the way the singers are forced to pronounce the name of the country they are addressing. It always comes out "Cana-duh." I dont know whether that is a meaningful observation or not.

I always thought the purpose of a national anthem was to promote solidarity and patriotism. "O Canada" seems intent on disqualifying most of the people who live here.

The schoolteachers and civil servants who wrote the English words to our ballpark song should have checked out the enthusiasm for that inclusive anthem you can still hear around Toronto: "Okay, Blue Jays, let's play ball!"

A Professional Writer Temp

AYBE IT WAS MY MOTHER's fault that I became a professor as well as a writer. In our family she had the job of instilling puritanism in her kids. I finished high school and spent a hitch in the air force and started college in the fifties. The fifties was a decade of opposites. The media-trend people tend to remember it as residential driveways and Louis St. Laurent. But we who were hormonal at the time recall Marlon Brando and Elvis Presley, dangerous talent and doom.

Half of me wanted to live the romantic life of a novelist such as those encountered in the novels of the time, and half of me just somehow gave in to the idea of responsibility. I never planned to become a university professor in the sixties, but somehow I kept going to school, and the longer you go to school the more likely you will be a professor.

So I learned to write lyric poems and bits of novels and stuff in those few moments when I was not marking papers or preparing classes or caretaking the apartment building we lived in, or, later, mowing my own damned lawn. Here's what I told myself: you could be a writer, or you could be a professor, or you could go to work. Being a professor might not be as good as being a writer, but it was better than going to work.

Once in a while I got a Canada Council grant or a sabbatical, and I could be a writer for a year. By this time I was married and had a credit card and eventually a mortgage, so the writing life was not very romantic, in the sense of garrets and sidewalk cafes. But man, it was nice to get up every day and attack that book. In 1992 I had one of those years, and I used it writing a novel called *Shoot!* I also kept a diary of the writing of the novel, as if I were a regular novelist.

People tell me that if I am such a prolific writer, I must

be extraordinarily disciplined. I dont feel as if I am. I have been lazy all my life, or so the puritanism learned from my mother has always told me. The writer who really figured out how to be productive though a professor is Hugh Hood. He routinely worked every day of the summer break and every day of the winter space between semesters, and produced a really long shelf of novels and short stories.

Nineteen ninety-two was one of the best years I ever had, the kind of year I had hoped I would have every year, when I could sit at my desk every day and make fiction. I had my second Canada Council senior grant. The first one I had used to work on a novel called *Burning Water*. I never had a Canada Council junior grant. I didnt think that I was good enough to apply at first, and then when I thought I was good enough, they told me that I was an accomplished writer, so it was too late to get one.

Now, when your Canada Council year comes to an end, you are supposed to write a letter to the council, reporting on yourself. Here is the sort of stuff you write to them:

Thank you for making that year possible. I hope I will justify your faith. I am known as a puritanical worker, but I always feel as if I could be doing a lot more. Well, I did not spend the time being creative in Spain or Greece, the way (so I was told then) CC artists used to a few decades past. I spent my time in my study at home, in libraries and museums and archives, on Indian reserves, in old mines, on ranches and mountaintops in the Interior of this province and across the line.

As you know, my plan was to research and write a novel that acts as a kind of "prequel" to my 1987 novel, *Caprice*, based on the sad story of the McLean family from the Kamloops area over a hundred years ago. I started my research on January 2, 1992, sharing days between it and the other writing tasks I had promised that I would do, a

10,000-word autobiography for a U.S. academic publisher, the two last stories in a story collection, two book reviews, et cetera. I researched and researched, as one has to do when one saddles oneself with a novel set 110 years ago. On May 1, I decided to start writing while continuing to research. By December 31, on which day I wrote 750 words, I had 246 pages of typescript. (To show how one's production suffers when one has to teach at a university, I now have 263 pages of typescript.) Two hundred and forty-six pages come to about 65,000 words. I am writing without extravagance. The words come charingly.

I am fortunate to have a friend named Dwight Gardiner. Many years ago he was a student of mine in Montreal. Now he is a linguist whose specialty is the Salish language of the Shuswap people around Kamloops. He works up there, and in fact often teaches there, at the former residential school (which figures often in my earlier novel) that is now the Indian educational centre. Dwight knows, after several years of working with them, many of the Shuswap and Okanagan elders, and a lot of the younger people. I was fortunate that while I was up there doing geographical and archival investigations, I could tag along with Dwight and his associate, and spend time in the homes of elders at several communities. I was able to funnel my questions about history and folkways and such through Dwight. Sometimes the findings were a delight. I am thinking of Okanagan elder Herb Manuel at Douglas Lake, for instance, who confirmed a theory about Indian migration I had formulated after reading the (probably) fiction of Mourning Dove, the native writer from the Colville reservation in Washington. This entailed a legend of Athabaskan speakers from Oregon country migrating into the Nicola Valley after a peculiar dispute about the way a flying goose makes noise in the air. Well, it is the beginning of a story that would use up all your time. It will be in the novel, in any case.

I visited, several times, the museums in Ashcroft, Cache Creek, Kamloops, Merritt, et cetera, the McLean ranch in Hat Creek, which is the birthplace of some of my characters, and the actual cabin near Douglas Lake, where they were captured by the law. That was a lucky event. I was told how to get there, if I would keep it quiet, from the Kamloops historian Mel Rothenburger, who is the son of a friend of my mother and a great-grandchild of one of the McLeans. And so on. In Okanagan, Washington, I had an actual semi-mystical experience, some agency leading me directly to the grave of Mourning Dove, after the people at the Omak tourist bureau told me they had never heard of her. I gave them particulars and showed them some of my books. In the dinky little nineteenth-century mining town of Wallace, in the mountains of Idaho, I went into a dumb little second-hand bookstore and found a book I had just about given up hope of seeing. While I was there I went with an extended family to a lonely mountain shack and buried the ashes of an old friend, the great U.S. fiction writer Douglas Woolf, who first inspired me to write about the Indian-labour things I am writing about now.

The books are still piled up, along with the photocopied microfilm newspapers. The used file cards are in a Haida thunderbox my wife bought me for Christmas, and the piles of unused-so-far file cards are piled in piles in front of my printer. Letters fly out of the house and other letters migrate into it. Rolls of film turn into pictures of ranches and mountain valleys. The 1979 story and the 1992 story take place in the hills where I worked as a Merritt-based forest service tree-marker and cruiser in 1958. I met the Nicola chief, Dan Manuel, and was alarmed: he looks just like his father, old Daniel Manuel, whom I knew thirty-five years ago.

I plucked up my nerve and went to visit Jeanette Armstrong at the Enokw'in Centre in Penticton. She heard me out and told me that she already knew about my project.

Maybe she was on a Canada Council jury or knew someone on a Canada Council jury. I told her that I was sensitive to the misappropriation of voice issue, at least as it applies to First Nations people, because my study has told me that the Okanagan and Shuswap people, for instance, value invisible property over visible property. I have learned a great deal about Indian people and half-breed people (so far the word *métis* is used here only academically) in the last year. I know a hundred times more history of the valley I grew up in. It took me a year to find out that the important Indian bitterroot is what we kids in Oliver, B.C., called rock rose. Anyway, I told Jeanette that any stories I refer to will be credited. One of the elders I spent hours with this summer in Chase, Mary Arnoose, died in the fall. Already.

I have often remarked to people that I would like to get out of literature and spend the rest of my life studying the native people of the great interior plateau. I am sure that I will spend some of my time doing that. I am going to deliver a paper on Mourning Dove at the Learned Societies meeting in June.

When will I finish the first draft of this novel? I wont be able to work on it every day of the week till May again. I originally thought that this would be a three-hundred-page typescript. I have lately come to realize that I am looking at four hundred. I hope to have a draft by September 1, 1993. There will be a chapter in the B.C. issue of *Books in Canada* (May), and now *Quarry* has asked me for some of the work in progress as well. Gad, I wish I were on another year of the CC grant!

In any case, you will know about it when I have it ready. A certain publisher has told someone else that he knows about the McLean brothers and is interested in seeing what I do with them. He may hate the latter. But at least he will get the first look. Thank you again for the wonderful chance to do the work instead of just dreaming about it.

It is interesting to me to read that letter again after a few years, if only to see that I was trying to appear as if I were a humble dynamo of some sort, a kind of lazy puritan.

One day in Toronto, sitting in a cafeteria at Eaton's, I went over the manuscript with my editor, working as fast as possible because the cafeteria was closing and I had a plane to catch. I dont know whether it helped or hurt that David McFadden, the travel writer, was kibitzing as we worked. Here is what we did: we threw out a hundred pages of a five-hundred-page manuscript, said our goodbyes, and went our various ways, she down to her lakeside office, I to the airport. This, I told myself, dazzled as always by the big publishing world in Toronto, is the romantic life of the novelist.

Random-Access Coach House

ONE DAY I OFFERED MY SKULL to Ann Hungerford. She is a playwright and language teacher who had been experimenting on writers' brains. She theorized that writers initiate their work variously—some hear language, some see language, and some work out of a kind of abstraction the more logical among us would call logical. I was reminded of Ezra Pound's maintaining in his *ABC of Reading* that superior writers coordinate "phanopoeia, melopoeia, logopoeia."

Late one Friday afternoon Ann led me to a laboratory full of electro-imagic equipment. There she and others attached three dozen electrodes to my cranium. These were also attached to a box hanging from my neck, which in turn led to a computer in another room, on which appeared an electroencephalographic screen. I, on the other hand, was placed before an IBM computer. I had been using Apples and Macintoshes longer than most writers had been wired, but I had never touched an IBM before. The writing program was Microsoft Word, which I use all the time. But I saw that I was going to have to relearn the business of making things happen without windows and a mouse.

Here is what I was supposed to do: sit and write on the IBM computer for several hours, while Ann in the other room scanned my brainwaves. I did. I wrote the first portion of an experimental (it seemed appropriate) poem. I wrote some other stuff. Then typing as fast as I could, but still not gleaning my teeming brain, I wrote out some unordered memories of Coach House Press.

For those who dont know, Coach House Press had been since the mid-sixties the principal publisher of avant-garde writing in English Canada. For those who know that but who have not been keeping track, there was eventually a new regime at Coach House Press made of people who were not around during the revolution and who wanted the press to be respectable.

A few months later Ann brought me a printout of what I had written. The verse will find its way into print some time. Some of the stuff will just disappear like most brainwaves. Here will follow a few of my unordered memories of Coach House Press, which received a manuscript from me via bp Nichol in 1965, and published it in 1967. I published a career's worth of books with CHP.

When Coach House Press published *Geneve* in 1971, my tarot poem, they used Angela's tarot pack for a photograph that was printed on the inside of the dust jacket on the clothbound version. In the photograph the cards (the major arcana) are laid out in a spiral, in the order in which they appear in the book, upon an Oriental rug with spiralling patterns. Quite a number of people reading the book did not have the Curiosity (heh) to unwrap the book and look at the picture inside. Others, once they found the picture, removed the dust jacket from the pumpkin-coloured cloth, unfolded it, and put it on their walls as a non-poetry poster.

After the publication of the book, CHP didnt bother to get the tarot pack back to me, but stored it, wrapped in its silk square, as is the proper custom, on a shelf in the main lounge or whatever that upstairs room is called at Coach House, along with the archive of books and magazines constructed at the press. Hundreds of workers, writers, vagrants, and friends of the family would hang around in that room over the years. What odds.

I guess it must have been something like seven years after *Geneve* came out, after we had moved to Vancouver, that I found the cards, still there, at the press. Actually, I think that it was more like ten years, but seven years always works quite well in narratives such as this. I picked them up, along with a bunch of recent Coach House books. One could, if one were a CHP author, still do that in those days. Postcards and poesy, try to figure out where to pack them, as always, for the flight back across the Rockies. Reading new poetry on a new jet west across the new world. *L'étoile.*

The cards are now in Angela's study, but I dont remember whether they are still wrapped in silk. They are several rooms from the nearest copy of *Geneve.*

I was there in the old narrow brick building on the lane behind Huron Street shortly after Coach House Press got its own perfect binder. A perfect binder makes those books whose pages are trimmed neatly on the right and glued to the spine on the left or vice versa. The CHPers treated it in what used to be the time-honoured Coach House manner.

Everything that was not nailed down was being perfect-bound. Blank-paged books appeared with exotic covers, often covers of Coach House books. Nurse novels sported covers from Northrop Frye texts. A book by Michael Ondaatje had a Canadian cigarette box as its wrapping.

They mixed and matched, the eclectic crew. It was beautiful. It was also learning. It had a trace of 1967, of Rochdale and the origins of the Coach House Press. Young people were finding out, their hands on the machine, how to do something, while persuading themselves that they were having the kind of fun that people who were not tokers and longhairs and wives and husbands who were not taken in by the slick city magazines later decades would never see or understand. And if that is a funny sentence, so what?

I mean no one even bothered to think like numismatics. No one made a Margaret Atwood book with a perfect bill bissett cover just so that they could sell it to a collector in

1999. I dont think anyone did. I hope not. No, I am nearly sure no one did.

But I am typing this with a bunch of EEG wires in my head, and typing on an IBM machine for the first time, and listen, there is more—it has red letters on the white buzz of a screen, and no mouse. EEK. I have to relearn how to be a second-generation computer freak.

The Coach House people were first-generation computer freaks as far as the Canadian publishing scene was concerned. I mean that head freak Stan Bevington used to get LIP grants and OFY grants, and a lot of that money would go into the purchase of amazing new machines in the offices upstairs, up above the old iron hand press and the huge typesetting machine, that monster metal spider that threw hot lead through the air, past the humming head of Victor Coleman, bent before it, his spatulate fingers making beautiful lines of 1968 verse. How I miss those times.

I reflect now. What kind of writing do I want this to be, I with these wires in my scalp, cult cyber-horror movie anti-hero. Do I want to see sections of a piece on Coach House Press, fit them together, make a possible paper of them, read them to the Curious (there he goes again) in the side room at the National Library in hot humid Ottawa? Or does this person, android skull face, want to reflect on CHPress, offer you poetry of the metrical age, the metre a cable under the sea of this old gink's islanded brain?

If that was truly a question, I will stand with that question mark. After all, I am typing more than I generally do on a Friday afternoon.

Trying to imPress whom? No, trying to make a piece, to escape from the evasion of writing I have been doing at home these afternoons this whole week.

I feel as if I have a hat on.

Or a hat inside my cranium bone, whew.

Anyway, the computers at CHP. They kept provoking articles with pictures and personalities in the big daily press, including the *Globe and Mail*, probably even the business pages. Bearded gink in this dot-dot picture looks like a Doukhobor tractor-fixer, got a screen in front of his face, a gleam behind his eyeglasses, what used to be expertise regarding burning herbs now converted to this PAL program, whew again. I mean, I remember Stan on the subway, sitting there on the sideways seat, eyes straight ahead, two big paper sacks beside his feet in boots, a Doukhobor hat on his head, round crown.

Eventually all your books will be on the screen, inside the chips only. If there is such a thing as print, it will just be collectors' beautiful artifacts. Who better to do that than Coach House Press?

I mean, do you remember those 1968 posters they used to make for rock-and-roll concerts outdoors at Varsity Stadium? Remember that you could not read them unless you were stoned, and then you probably only thought you could read them, because if anyone asked you what they were about, you would just mumble words or parts of words. Like Chet Baker thinking he can really play really gone when he is high up through his own bony brain.

Varsity Stadium, oh yes. Once there was a three-day rock festival there, lots of the hot groups, their names filled two columns of print, from what was it, 1969? Vanilla Fudge? The Who? Procul Harem. The Kinks. I went free, but not much. And if the statute of limitations permits, here is how I went free.

Some narcorevolutionary love heads at CHP had got hold of a pair of tickets for the three-day festival of decibels, and applied guerrilla hipster logic to the situation, that musicapitalism right across the street nearly, in the DMZ.

They found similar paper and ink and type and so on, and printed a fair number of tickets for the festival. The listeners would be in the stands and on the grass of the football field, after all, and there was room for everyone.

It was amazing to hand the ticket to a tough guy at the gate and walk right in.

The music was loud and sort of like San Francisco. There is no way to tell younger people, people the age of the new crowd at Coach House, what feeling passed between the air and the human interior in those days. The summer was hot and humid. The folks were wearing clothes like buccaneers in fifties movies. Some may even have had sabres between their teeth. Some of the rock singers sounded as if they did. I think Donovan was there. You could understand his words, if you wanted to.

So in the crowd were a lot of people with tickets with the same serial numbers on them, but no guard noticed. Of course not. This was one of the japes the "movement" could be proud of during that period when entrepreneurs were trying to make a bundle off the populace's appetite for the counterculture. I was not a great rock fan, though I once drank the Ottawa night away on roadsides with the Youngbloods, and so on. I was into ESP jazz records, Albert Ayler and his brother Don, as taught to me by Greg Curnoe of London and John Sinclair of Detroit.

Oh, this IBM screen is doing idiosyncratic things. Now I have a black rectangle whose length keeps changing, right after my last red words, and often letters just dont make it onto the screen anyway. Ann says that something like that is happening to the brainwave monitor.

A few weeks later there was a rock concert, as they were starting to call them, because this music after "Sergeant Pepper" was acquiring pretensions, at Maple Leaf Gardens. Coach House spies got a couple of tickets and reproduced a certain number of them again. This time, though, the tickets were larger in number than the available seats in the hockey arena, and after a while the guards were eager to read the figures on the ducats. There was not a lot of elbow room in Maple Leaf Gardens. I am glad that I wasnt there. I think the Doors were on the program anyway.

The only time I have been inside Maple Leaf Gardens was the occasion on which two other Coach House authors and I bought some tickets off a scalper and saw the Leafs beat Detroit 6–0. They were at the time very unsuccessful teams. After the game was over, David McFadden, whose ticket I had bought, announced that he would like to read his poems aloud to whomever stayed in their seats. The other author, David Young, disappeared from sight.

One time I was being old familiar George, you never know when he's going to appear all at once, loud at the press, come first thing in Toronto to the lane behind Huron Street, stomp loudly up the stairs, give them the familiar twice a year, say, surprise. Loud guy from the West Coast but an old pal of the press, first book in Centennial Year, remember?

This time I slammed the bottom door, or maybe I did, and stomped really loud up those narrow worn-down wooden steps, headed for the scarred familiar table and good coffee. They were going to be as always glad to see me.

Really loud, making some loud remark, as if in the middle of a cross-the-street conversation, here I am from the cool Pacific, noisy.

But it is a little embarrassing, or a middle amount embarrassing. Because there's Stan Bevington at the table with papers and photos all over its surface, and two or was it three guys in suits no matter the weather in consultation. These were, I think, ginks from the National Gallery, who were talking with Stan about publishing a lucrative picture book through the press.

Whew, I suddenly became a quieter guy, said I will just look around, see what's new, talk with Nelson and the boys.

That's all the Coach House memoiring I have from this occasion. I had intended to tell the story of Stan Bevington and the acid and the book in the fishbowl. As a matter of fact, I thought that I had typed this one out. Maybe it got lost among the chips. Maybe it strayed between the brainwaves. Maybe I mixed intention with typing.

Anyway, it was really late Friday afternoon, or more properly, evening. We were both tired, and Ann knew that it was going to take more than an hour to get the electrodes off my head and the conducting gel out of my hair. We were both brain-tired, so we quit for the night.

The stuff I got could have been better, but I am not overly displeased by the words the experience called up at ski-jump speed. Maybe if I get used to the IBM and the electrodes and the necessity to keep kind of still, I can make a better second instalment of memoirs. As Ezra Pound put it in *ABC of Reading*: "The best work probably does pour forth, but it does so AFTER the use of the medium has become 'second nature,' the writer need no more think about EVERY DETAIL, than Tilden needs to think about the position of every muscle in every stroke of his tennis."

Ann, meanwhile, hasnt told me whether she saw anything while she was looking at the brain monitor.

Theft in the Afternoon

T HE MOST COMMON bumper sticker in Spain those days showed an orange circle, which, when you got as close as most Spanish drivers do, appeared to be a world, and the message "Sevilla '92." As anyone knows, the year 1492 was pretty important in Spain, so on the five hundredth anniversary Spain got the Olympics (Barcelona) and the world's fair (Seville).

When we were children the oranges we ate were likely to have the word "Seville" printed on them. One has always associated Seville with the bullfight and oranges. Well, today in the restaurants of all the nice hotels in Seville you will ask for orange juice and get Tang. You can, on summer Sundays, get bull.

Situated in Andalucía, the old Moorish south of Spain, and yet not on the Costa del Sol, which is now hundreds of kilometres of high-rise apartment buildings, Seville is probably the prettiest large city in Spain. The river whose name you can never remember cools the high heat, and there are trees everywhere, including dark green ones from which you can pluck oranges if you like. Even death in the afternoon is pretty. The bullring in Seville is the second most important one in the country and by far the nicest looking.

The jasmine and the bougainvillea can lull you, make you drift, lift you into a haze of loveliness and excess. That is an unfortunate irony, because Seville is a city in which you should be alert and extra alert at all times.

Here is the reason for your alertness: in all of Europe, Seville is the most famous city for thieves. There are very good thieves in Lyon and in Sicily, but the Seville thieves would rob them blind. When the world's fair came to Seville in 1992, the Spanish theft of the Aztec and Inca treasures looked like petty shoplifting at a lemonade stand.

Some people point out that while the unemployment rate in Spain is 22 per cent, in Seville it is 37 per cent, and that is the reason for the high crime rate. But nineteenth-century travellers learned to be extra careful there in the paradisal drift. There are a lot of ways to be ripped off. In *The Dangerous Summer*, Hemingway wrote: "Neither of us cared truly for Sevilla. This is heresy in Andalucía and in bull-fighting. People who care about bullfighting are supposed to have a mystic feeling about Sevilla. But I had come to believe over many years that there are more bad bullfights there in proportion to those given than in any other city."

It is possible to have a mystic feeling about Seville. La Giralda, the Moorish tower in the middle of the city, is the tallest in Spain. People in Spain's other cities are supposed to envy the Sevillanos their perfumed stroll through life. Bizet's Carmen lived there, and so did Mozart's Don Giovanni. The cathedral is the largest Gothic building in the world, and the third-largest church in Christendom. Christopher Columbus, who travelled almost as much after death as he had in life, is buried there. Parts of him, anyway.

But if you walk around the cathedral and the nearby Barrio Santa Cruz, a maze of narrow twisty streets that afford marvellous views of homeowners' wrought-iron, blue tile, and potted-palm doorways, you had better do so without a purse or bag or open pocket.

Let us imagine a middle-aged, much-travelled Canadian poet and/or novelist walking along Calle Aire in the Barrio Santa Cruz, returning to his hotel after the little get-acquainted stroll he customarily takes while waiting for his wife and daughter to unpack and arrange their cosmetics and accessories. Let us, for convenience, call him George. In Spanish that would be Jorge, or Tonto. He wears a shoulder bag, but he is being careful. He has the strap over his right shoulder and the bag at his left hip. He has his left hand on the bag. Inside the bag is his wallet, his Swiss Army knife, and all the other stuff. In a semi-secret pocket are all his traveller's cheques.

In front of him he sees the French couple from his hotel. Each of them is wearing a shoulder bag hanging straight off one shoulder. Not very smart. In one more block everyone will be back at the hotel. The French couple, arriving at the last fork in the labyrinth, turns left. Jorge turns right. He can see the square on which the hotel fronts.

All over Europe, in every city of Spain, and especially here in Seville, there are noisy little motor scooters. Motor scooters do not cost as much as cars do, so youths whose income depends on the hunting conditions can get them. They are also good for narrow winding streets and parking.

Now a youth on a motor scooter appears in the light where narrow Calle Aire meets the square. Jorge moves toward the wall on his right to make room for the motor scooter. It makes a loud noise and picks up speed. Jorge feels the strap of his bag ripped away.

Oh, he thinks, the guy got his rear-view mirror caught in my strap. He is spinning and nearly falling, Jorge. Then he sees the parallel between his situation and the warnings in the best travel books, the stories about other people that can never happen to you because you have been everywhere.

Jorge is filled with sickening frustration. He feels as if something is all over. Later he will be told that he feels as if he has been raped. He sees the youth turning to look at him with no expression in his face.

Seville is very beautiful, but after you have been robbed you just want to get out of town. You might even say to someone that you want to get out of Andalucía, or Spain. But first you have to spend a whole evening and night at the Central Precinct of the Guardia, where they are very rude to you and where they already know what has happened and how. There you will talk for hours with Germans and French people and others who have had their car windows smashed by thieves who were being watched by police, or so the victims will tell you. You know that you will never get your stolen property back, but you will not be able to drive any more, or apply for replacement traveller's cheques without a police document.

Then you will spend all the next day in some travel agencies, trying to get your replacement traveller's cheques. Perhaps you will be lucky, or perhaps, like Jorge, you will be told to pick them up in Lisbon, no problem, and then later in Lisbon you will be told after waiting in the office for a few hours that they do not know what you are talking about, but that is all right, you will get them back home in Vancouver, no problem, is it not?

Still, Seville is a lovely-looking city, a perfect setting for the broken female hearts left in Don Juan's trail. It is certainly more beautiful than Brisbane, where the 1988 world's fair was perpetrated. If you were a fan of world's fairs, you already had your reservations for Brisbane. If you planned to attend Sevilla '92, you thought about wearing a money belt and not renting a car. You thought you might just stay in a hotel with a lobby safety vault.

But you knew that you would start every meal with gazpacho, the marvellous cold soup made in a great variety of ways out of tomatoes, cucumbers, and onions. They would never be able to take that away from you.

On Not Teaching the Véhicule Poets

$\mathcal{E}$ NGLISH-LANGUAGE CREATIVE writing students in Montreal of the late sixties and early seventies, if they were serious about things, were up against a number of problems. English-language poetry in Quebec had a history that was both nationally known and insular. As far as the Montreal flacks and interested partisans in the rest of Canada were concerned, Irving Layton was the big poet of his generation, and Leonard Cohen was the big poet of the next generation. Young poets looking for glamour in a poetry career were either enamoured of Cohen's example or obstructed by it. Young poets looking for poetry were not given much of a chance to find it outside the local legends.

Put it another way: there were, according to Montreal literary scenarists, two major traditions of Eng-lang poetry, the Anglo line of Scott, Smith, Kennedy, Jones, and the magazines like *Northern Review*, and the Jewish bunch led by Layton, but including Cohen (sort of) and the Laytonettes, Boxer, Hertz, Mayne, et cetera. Neither crowd was particularly noted for keeping up with what was happening in the U.S. and Canada. The Montreal world, self-inflated, was sufficient to itself. As will happen in such a situation, attention was deflected away from form and technique and directed toward personality and portrayal of the homeland.

The best antidote to such provincialism was the poetry reading series at Sir George Williams University, which started the year before I got there. It was organized by Roy Kiyooka, the prominent poet/painter who was teaching at SGWU at the time, and English professors Stan Hoffman and Howard Fink. Compared to the desultory reading series run at universities in later days, it was a class act. The poets were flown to Montreal, met at the airport, lodged at the Ritz-Carlton Hotel, given lots of attention and room service, a dinner, the reading, and a party that was not BYO anything. There were ten or twelve poets a year featured in that series, including Robert Duncan, John Newlove, Michael McClure, Margaret Avison, George Oppen, and Daphne Marlatt. I have not seen its like in the three decades since then.

I assumed then and assume now that the opportunity created by that reading series did more for "my" writing students than anything I could have told them. But I did tell them a lot. I told them which poets and books I found it important to read. I told them how to make poems from language instead of attitude. I told them that if you had $2.10 to your name, you could buy a book of David McFadden's poetry for $1.95.

After I left Montreal in 1971, a bunch of young poets and other miscreants started a reading series at Véhicule Gallery, and a press called Véhicule. Since that time, hyperactive Ken Norris has been keeping the name in whatever part of the public eye turns to poesy in and around Montreal. The Véhicule people got a good thing going, and certainly filled a gap that existed in English-language poetry in Quebec.

I had had some of the Véhiculae in my writing classes at Sir George.

I didnt know what I was getting myself into, a westerner with definite opinions about poetry and its sources, dropped into the middle of Layton country. Well, there was Louis Dudek, who did not quite fit into the Anglo tradition, and who was not a Jewish poet, though people often thought he was. He had been for a few decades a magazine publisher, culture critic, and very unornamental modernist poet. He sat on couches in Anglo apartments and Jewish apartments. He had published Leonard Cohen and Lionel Kearns. When I arrived in Montreal a famous quarrel between Dudek and Layton was still raging.

But I didnt see Louis any more often than I saw everyone else. Everyone else saw everyone else, among the published, and that included me. But out of my habitual element, I was taken aback when I went to their parties only to hear that they discussed everything but poetry.

So my creative writhing (as Newlove called it) classes. With my memory shot now, I cannot remember all the young poets I sat with, and sometimes I like to think that I had students, Endre Farkas, for instance, who probably never sat in my room. I know some of the people I subjected to the heat: Carl Law, Tom Konyves, Dwight Gardiner, Susan Landell, Tom McAuley, Artie Gold.

Dwight Gardiner and Artie Gold were two hotshot friends, both going bald in their early twenties, both wry and hip. I was pleased to see that of all things, they were both reading Jack Spicer and Frank O'Hara. In 1966 I had had to introduce Spicer to the hip poetry gang in Detroit! Now a year or two later, I find two kids who had found him and O'Hara somewhere. Wonderful. Because not only were Spicer and O'Hara obviously in the underground as compared to the poets known by professors and big presses—they were even the contrary found in that underground. They were a challenge to Olson and Creeley, and so on. Wonderful.

Of course Gardiner published four books before he became an ethnolinguist among the Shuswap people in the Thompson Valley. Gold published four books in his youth, and then became a middle-aged Selected Poet of the disappearing kind. In my classes Artie Gold would arrive every week with two huge bags—one containing enough food to get him through to mid-class break and the other crammed with a couple hundred new poems. When it came to photocopying the students' poems for class argument, it was sometimes like pulling hens' snot to get material from some of the hobbyists and explorers of self, but it was like putting up a snow fence against an avalanche of Artie.

Tom Konyves was a sly European, offspring of big-city Hungarian Jews, a touch of another kind of maturity in the long room. He knew he was a poet or something, but he didnt know whether what he wanted to make was poems. I told him that form was never more than an extension of something or other, and the materials he handed in were less and less comfortable on the page. My conservative side rose up to resist, always a good sign. Konyves started making things out of the paper itself. Then he started substituting for paper. Then he threw away his pen. I recognized his restless genius and said get out of here.

A few years later he got tired of reading that Pound's "In a Station of the Métro" was a perfect modernist poem. He got a bunch of poets down to a station of the Montreal métro, the busiest crossroad on the line, and had them perform the poem there, for hurrying strangers who hurried by in many east-end languages. All the while he videotaped the event. Last I heard he is a video doyen in Vancouver, still interested in poetry, but not poems all that much.

Endre Farkas, a jovial European, child of rural Hungarian Jews, would become a publisher as well as a poet, and he would eventually sidle toward the stage, writing libretti for operas and collaborating with dance companies. He, like Gold, would eventually enter middle age, somewhat white-haired, somewhat bald. Like Louis Dudek. Dudek became the champion of Ken Norris, a little bespectacled fellow, who kept getting married and divorced, splitting his time between Maine and the South Pacific, and producing books of poems by the carton.

The other Tom, i.e., McAuley, was a lot quieter than those guys. He was steady and productive. His poems became longer and more pared down as he progressed. I didnt say a lot to him, or I didnt say it very loud. I recognized a quiet, dedicated poet, a man who wanted to spend his life making poems better and better. I have met a few poets like that around the country, people like David Phillips and Judith Copithorne. We dont know how much we need them.

I didnt teach creative writhing any more, or rather I did so only one semester after leaving Montreal in 1971. I think that maybe we all have jobs we can be expected to do *for a while*—edit magazines, review books, teach writing classes. Creative writing teachers are always quick to tell you they once had so-and-so in a class. Hell, Earle Birney used to say he had *me* in a class. That's all right, but it should never be confused with influence or shaping of careers or anything like that. If I had anything to do with the emergence of Véhicule, I will gladly acknowledge the acknowledgement.

But there are other memories of that Sir George writing course. Like the time I did something I couldnt imagine myself doing—telling a noisy troublemaker to get out of my class and never come back. Whew! Or the time Susan Landell's chair fell over backward with a hell of a clatter. Sure woke us up.

I'm surprised that Tom Konyves didnt work it into one of his poetry readings.

Laughing at Grads

IN THE SPRING, OR WAS it the fall, I forget—it was 1994, anyway, the University of British Columbia gave me an honorary degree and asked me to address a gymnasium full of young people in square hats. For the occasion I wore the Three Stooges tie my daughter had given me for my birthday. When it came time to be photographed with the president of the university and the chancellor of the university, I made sure that my jacket was open and my gown back on my shoulders so you could see the tie.

At the president's residence there was a reception for me and Jane Rule, who was also getting an honorary degree. But I got stuck in the students' bar on the other side of the campus. My old high school friend Billy Martino was there, and so was his youngest son, who had just got his degree in something, something in the arts. All of Billy's other sons were jocks, as Billy was. One of them was a professional football kicker. But this one was interested in poetry, and I think that Billy was as glad to get him together with me as he was to get his other sons together with the scouts. So Billy kept buying another round of beer, and though I frequently announced that I had a reception to get to, I thought it would be impolite to leave with a pint glass half full. As it turns out, I was pretty swacked when I finally found the president's residence, and for sure now I could not pronounce that phrase. The last guests were leaving. I felt a certain definite disapproval. It was a feeling I was familiar with from high school, various jobs, and my days in the air force.

But earlier, when I was sober, I had made a pretty good impression on the students with my speech, and no parents or UBC officials had tried to stop me. The speech went something like this:

*Graduation day—what a wonderful day it is for photography
shops! You people getting ready to commence your real lives might
be looking at a world that is not falling all over itself to offer you a
job. Maybe you should open a photography shop. Look around today.
You will see all kinds of people standing still in their funny hats and
long robes while parents try to remember how their cameras work.
Or those little TV cameras. This would not be a good day to pick
your nose—you'll probably be on camera. For years and years
Jessica's family will be looking at Jessica's graduation tapes, and
someone will say, "Look at that guy in the funny hat. In a second
he starts picking his nose."*

*Why are all these people taking pictures of students at
convocation? It could be that the pictures are going to be
what parents get back after all those years of shelling out. It
could be that they cant quite believe that their dumb kid
could actually get through university. A colour picture on the
mantel is proof.*

*It could be for laughs. Graduation pictures are always funny.
People look back at their own graduation pictures or those of their
generation and laugh their heads off. Most of the hilarity has to do
with hair. "Oh my God!" people say, looking at their graduation
pictures. In the pictures from the fifties all the guys' ears stick
straight out because they didnt have any hair on the sides of
their head. In the early sixties the young women had towering
back-combed beehive hairdos. In the late sixties the guys had
huge Afros that looked like frozen hair explosions, or they had
long straight honky hair hanging down the fronts of their
graduation gowns. You know the rest: shaved heads, Mohawks,
green and purple hair. Twenty years from now you'll be looking
at your graduation pictures and tapes and hooting about earrings
on the guys and nose rings on the women.*

*Nothing wrong with that. It's only fashion. There wouldnt
be any fashion if you didnt laugh about yesterday's fashion.*

*But after you've laughed and your friends have laughed, you'll
still be looking at the pictures. You'll have an expression on your*

face that looks a bit like sadness. Call it wistful. You'll know that all that laughing at funny hair was to cover this feeling.

If you could turn things around, if on your graduation day you could look at photographs from twenty or forty years in the future, you would know what that feeling was. It is a mixture of nostalgia, regret, longing, pride, fondness, and pity. But those ingredients cannot define it. It is something like homesickness. Call it graduation sickness.

I hope your family is getting this all down on videotape. I know you're too caught up in your individual excitement and relief, even in a convocation, to catch or remember what this old fart up here is saying. I didnt get to my own convocation because I had a job, picking cherries in the South Okanagan Valley, and I dont have any graduation pictures. But I remember what it felt like to finish that university degree at last. Kind of insecure, isnt it? There's a relief that you dont have to turn in an essay next week or the week after. But you're also not going to go to the caf or the pub with your regular friends after last class on Monday, either.

Have I got a reason for saying all this stuff? Is there a point I am trying to make? I have been wondering the same thing myself. I, too, am looking forward to the time when I can get this funny hat off and return the gown, though I wouldnt mind wearing it just once at the Waldorf beer parlour.

Well, I think that I am going to make a point, but it isnt going to come like bolt lightning through the roof. It starts like this: I can remember certain courses I took, and I can even remember particular days in particular classrooms, usually because something funny happened that day. Like the day when Professor Kato in Japanese literature forgot where he was and gave the whole lecture in French. We learnt more than usual that day because we had to pay attention harder.

Now I will tell you what happened while I was writing this little talk. As soon as I remembered Professor Kato and the French lecture, I remembered the day he sang a whole Noh drama, and the day we went to the tea house at Nitobe Garden and had a whole

Japanese meal, and this was years before Robson Street Japanese restaurants were invented. Then I started remembering hundreds of days at UBC, days that happened under specific weather more than thirty years ago, muchachos.

But a couple of days ago I sat in my kitchen and drank California champagne with a friend I went to UBC and the Georgia pub and jail with. He and I and another friend from UBC and my wife are writing a novel together. We live in three widespread places, but what are we writing about? We are writing about things that happened and things that by no means ever happened thirty-some years ago at UBC and off campus. And we are putting in hairdos to laugh at.

So that is my feeble little point. You never have to leave your university. Graduation happens gradually, commencement happens once, but convocation happens over and over. Stay here. Keep your friends. Chances are that in the future you wont be laughing at your hair—you'll be laughing at the lack of it or the colour of it.

And here's my hope for you: that when you are looking at your pictures and you have finished laughing at them, and you have that other expression on your faces, I hope you are spending a day with someone who was also there.

Parashoot!: Diary of a Novel

A LOT OF MY WRITING FRIENDS talk about the journals they keep. I dont keep a journal. I write a perfunctory diary, in which I keep my batting average and descriptions of the towns I travel to, maybe. I have a notebook in which I keep little abbreviated ideas for stories and essays and so on. But once in a while I hear about some writer (or more often some filmmaker) who keeps a journal about the book he is writing. So I tried it with my novel *Shoot!* It sort of worked, but, really, I found it hard to keep track of the difference between novel and diary of the novel. Have a look at some of the diary:

If you were an Indian in the Nicola Valley you would probably speak words from a number of languages, and after a while some of the languages would be white people's languages. If you were an Indian in that country in 1879, you would talk the way the Kamloops people talk, and the people up the river, too. You would know how to talk Okanagan and Chinook. Your talk would be injured by English words and French words the fur traders brought in. And then there were still some of the other words, the strange words the oldest Nicola people still had to use when they were telling their stories.

The old people would tell their stories, filled with those strange words.

"Yeh, yeh," you would say, and look serious, but some of those words would be words you only had to know for these stories.

Some of the stories were the truth and some of the stories were stories. Well, that was the way. The smartest people were the oldest people, and when they got to be old and told stories, they no longer cared if you said what is the truth and what is a story.

I wrote "By noon he was a corpse" in someone's cabin up on Tod Mountain, closed the little writing machine, and got into my Volvo.

That is, there is somebody writing all this. I was not going to mention that, or at least not often, meaning not to skew a reader's attention or even pleasure, until the following story happened.

It's a forty-five-minute drive from Tod Mountain to Kamloops. There, if you are going to town instead of the Sec^wepemc Centre, you cross one of the bridges over the Thompson. I crossed the main bridge, and instead of heading for an artery I took the quick right turn, a truck route. River Road, it said. Big machines clawing at the riverbank, dust in the air, detours, now this is more like it, I thought.

Around a detour, across from a beer bottle deposit, there was a little square park with a grass surface, elm trees on three sides, some kind of European pines along the fourth. A sign proclaimed Pioneer Cemetery. I stopped the Volvo and got out. In one corner of the park there is an L-shaped monument, old gravestones set side by side, horizontal now, in concrete. I looked at the grass again. There were rectangular patches of different-looking grass. There were slight depressions. Different colours. A peaceful-looking place, and deserted, only a few blocks from a mall filled with smoking teenagers.

I decided to see how many names I recognized in the L. There were some nineteenth-century storekeepers and their wives I knew. Hello, I said. Often there was the information given that the person mentioned was from Scotland. The names all sounded quite European.

Then I went for a little walk across the grass. Immediately

I came upon one grave all alone in the grass. There was the usual rectangle of stone or plaster or concrete, something hard, in any case, in the middle of the grass. And there was a flat horizontal grave marker. Here is what it proclaimed:

"In Memory of John T. Ussher—1844–1879—Killed by the McLean Bros."

Do you have a son about fifteen years old? What if a man with whisky on his breath put a black bag over his head and then put a thick bristly rope around his throat, fixed the thick knot under his ear, and pulled the lever that dropped the trap door under his slippered feet?

Here is the story Bill Arnouse told us at his kitchen table. One spring the people living in bear country had a guest from the south. The ice was gone in the river and the water was high and fast. The first insects had not yet arrived, and the sun was just warm enough to get the animals moving.

The guest from the south said he wanted to go for a walk to enjoy the spring sunshine and get the winter out of his legs.

"Dont do it," they told him. "This is bear country."

"Hell, I'm not afraid of bears," said the guest.

"We wouldnt go out there if we were you," said his hosts. "Stay around and we'll tell you some bear stories."

"I'm not interested in stories," said the guest. "If there's bears out there, I want to see the real thing."

So off he went. And sure enough, he hadnt got far from the cabin before he came up against a bear by the river. Well, it turned out he *was* afraid of bears, now that he'd seen one. He didnt care what kind of bear it was. He turned around and started running, and the bear took off after him, running the way bears run.

As the guest approached the cabin, running as fast as he could on the ground, he hollered, "Open the door!"

They opened the door all right, but just before the guest got there, he stepped to one side, and the bear went running right in through the door, fast. The guest slammed the door shut.

Then he hollered in through the shut door: "Skin that one, and I'll go get another!"

It was not a true story of the people. It was not a legend. It was just a tall tale. Wonderful bullshit.

Or maybe bearshit.

On a lovely warm day in July I drove my Volvo along the Nicola Valley and found the turnoff easily, partly because my friend in cowboy boots was driving a car in front of me. After a while the paved road became a dirt road. In the wide low sky ahead there were sparrow hawks swooping. Little birdhouses were affixed to fence posts. The famous historical creek appeared, from time to time, on our left.

My friend knew the people who lived up here but he did not know about the building I was looking for. On our way into the village I saw it. I recognized it immediately. It was more than a century later but there it was, the rough rectangular cabin sitting in high grass. Axe-hewn timbers with uneven space between them. Bullets in the wood.

We drove, as I had been advised, to the house across the road and got out. There were little kids in the yard and big kids on the porch. A car pulled into the drive and some adults got out. "I think I heard that's your cabin there," I said. "Aw-yup," he said. "I would be thankful if I could have permission to go and look at it, wont go inside," I said. "Sure," he said. He almost had a smile in his eyes.

"That's where the McLeans got captured," he said. I liked

that word. Better than *caught*. "Yeah," I said. "I'm glad there's no sign or anything. Some people came here once and wanted to make a sign," he said. "Dont let them," I said. "Awyup," he said.

So my friend in cowboy boots and I in light hiking shoes made our way around the fence and through the high grass. I went up very close and put my eye next to the bleached wood but I did not touch it with my fingers.

All along one of the end walls there were old branding irons hanging on nails. I had a good look at them. They were all the same brand, a big *S*.

Indian humour.

The Shuswap people had an old idea of law and order. Europeans liked to read newspapers and magazines about the wild Indians of the forest. They had mysterious ways, but they were essentially anarchic. They did not understand the laws of God and Queen and elector. They were afraid of Judge Begbie's rope.

But the Shuswap people understood law and order. The white people flooded into their valleys, and they seemed like nature gone bad. For the white people, law and order was a term made up to explain the way they could assign land to white people and assign Shuswap people to some other land they didnt want yet.

For the Shuswap people, land was where animals could be found. Law was about proprietary rights in animals. People lived in camps and moved according to the animals.

You do not throw a used deer bone into the river where the fish are. That is the law. You do not make war when it is time to kill a deer.

The white people wanted the skins off animals. They put them under the press and gave you a rifle for them. The Hudson's Bay Company had a charter. Nothing could be simpler. A charter is the opposite of the law.

No one in the Shuswap villages had ever been to Hudson's Bay.

Whenever I pass through dry country, big stones, few trees, maybe sagebrush and cactus, the thought comes to me that this is the way landscape is supposed to be, or this is the way God meant the world to look. Growing up in that kind of country, though, I read the Bible and other such books, and there it was, God's original plan, the garden of Eden. When Adam and Eve and all the rest of us got thrown out, it was into a kind of desert they got thrown. All through the Bible, whenever people are thrown out somewhere, it is always into the desert. Of course, where the Bible was written, just about all the country looks like the desert.

Where I grew up it looked a lot like the landscape in western movies. We played western movies a lot, with six-guns and all, but no horses. It helped a lot to be able to crouch with your six-gun behind a clump of real sagebrush. We wore neckerchiefs all the time. When we wanted something, we pulled the neckerchiefs up under our eyes.

I didnt think of it as landscape. It was just the valley and especially the hills. There were a lot of plants I didnt know the name of, but I recognized them. I knew where there were caves. I knew what spoor was, from the books I read after I got home in the dusk. I knew what coyote shit looked like.

My mother had an interesting attitude to my solo excursions. I would often come home with dried blood on my skin and hair and clothes, but she never went into a routine about it. She would notice and then go back to her activities, dumping coffee grounds out the window over the sink, for instance. I never broke a bone running the rock slides, but I lost quite a volume of blood over the years.

In fall of 1862 the Overlanders were travelling down the North Thompson River. They hadnt had anything to eat for several days. There was food all around them, but they did not know how to see it. They needed Indians to stay alive.

So they were really happy to see their first Indian village. They grinned in their scraggly beards, and shouted to each other as they brought their heavy rafts to shore and caught them up against the urgent water. They could not see any signs of life around the village.

So they walked up to the teepees and looked inside. They looked inside all of them. All they saw were dead bodies lying on the ground inside the teepees, lying next to one another, all ages.

The Overlanders did not even look around for food. They got out of the village as fast as they could.

Farther down the river they saw another Indian village and came close to the shore, but they did not see any signs of life in the village. They continued down the North River. They did not look at the Indian villages.

When they got to the South River they found some white men. In a few days they would begin to look around for useful land.

They thought all the Indians would disappear, and at least that sticky problem would go away. In places such as Victoria, people thought it was too bad, but perhaps the best thing overall, in the long run.

Many of the Shuswap people thought they would all disappear, too. They were filled with sadness. They were too tired to go out far into the mountains to bring back food and skins. Shuswap people wondered who had sent the white people.

The Cheyennes had a saying: "A nation is not conquered until the hearts of its women are on the ground."

The white men needed furs and food at first. Then they needed land and women. The white people kept sending their men across the ocean and leaving their women at home. The Shuswap and Okanagan men did not want to go across the ocean and help themselves to the spare white women. But the white men wanted women to do the kinds of jobs that seemed more like work than adventure. While they were at it, the white men also had someone other than each other and their horses to stick their penises into. But in the Shuswap and Okanagan communities there was not all that much time spent on war, so there was not a significant surplus of women.

It was a problem in arithmetic.

One day in the late sixties, a group of young Okanagan men arrived at a fairly new ranch at the north end of the big lake. All the wranglers were out in the hills, rounding up four-footed property. The Okanagan men went into every building and gathered every Okanagan woman in sight. They did not take anything else. They did not break anything or burn anything. They did not leave any feathered lances on a forty-five-degree angle in the dirt. There was a table with a nearly full bottle of Hudson's Bay whisky on it, and they just left it there. The dogs barked and snarled all around the feet of their horses, but they did not shoot any dogs. Hundreds of blackbirds were walking all over the manure on the vegetable patch, confident and industrious.

The Okanagan men put the Okanagan women on their horses. They made them leave all their cleaning utensils and sewing kits behind them. They wouldnt let them make the beds. The women did not make any noise. One of them was carrying a baby on a board at her back. That's the way the horses walked back home, clip clop.

While the Shuswap and Okanagan people were negoti-
ating their confederacy and scaring the pants off the
more recent occupants of the area, the Nez Percé people
a little to the south were at war with the United States
Army. This happened because white people located some
gold in the Salmon River and the Clearwater River on
the Nez Percé reservation. And wherever there is gold
there is timber, so in came the settlers, business as usual
on Indian ground.

Chief Joseph and his soldiers said enough is enough, and
so in 1877 they declared war on the United States. This
scared the pants off a lot of U.S. Americans, because Chief
Joseph's 250 soldiers fought to a draw with 500 bluecoats. A
lot of bluecoats and a lot of Nez Percé women and kids lost
their lives in Chief Joseph's war.

In Kamloops and Victoria they were reading about the
Nez Percé war.

Most people thought that eventually smallpox and other
European diseases would turn the Indian people into
history. But in the meantime you didnt want Indians on
the warpath.

The United States government reached an agreement
with Chief Joseph and his soldiers. The Nez Percé should
have known better. They thought they were going back to
the little bit that was left of their reservation. But the
U.S. government sent them to settle some malaria country
in Oklahoma, the former Indian Territory.

They read about that in Victoria.

It was getting harder to find skins for the Hudson's Bay
Company, and it was getting harder to find salmon for
the people. Sometimes when a Shuswap person went
to the river to find fish he would end up in the courtroom. He was guilty of trespassing. They told him what
they meant by trespassing, but who could understand

this language when the words in it did not mean what the things were? They said the cow people now owned the land beside the river. Sometimes they only leased the land in case their cows wanted to walk over there. If a Shuswap fisherman walked on that land to get to the river, he was guilty of trespassing.

It was as hard to understand as the sin. The priests came to the village every year and talked about the sin. They made a bad smell and a bad noise and talked in their language about the sin. They did not explain trespassing. They wanted fish, too.

When the priests made their buildings they took water into them, and they took Shuswap babies into the buildings and put water on their faces. Water which the salmon had passed through. They did not know what they were doing. When the white people made babies inside Shuswap women they did not know what they were doing.

It was not trespass or sin, because they did not wind up in a courtroom and they did not have to give things to the priests and their buildings.

They did not see some Shuswap people walking across cow country to paint pictures on stones.

The first batch of the famous historical Overlanders numbered thirty-five men and one woman. It made sense in a way. What would women be doing at such dangerous work? You head out into uncharted and ferocious land, not knowing what you might meet up with. You could only put faith in your instinct that nature would provide.

"Some day," said J. A. Mara, "someone will tell the story of the great adventure we are making in this country."

He was sitting on the wide veranda of his grand house overlooking a cluster of steep-roofed clapboard buildings beside the slow green river. This was little Kamloops, a town that could have been done away with in an hour by four men with torches. There was no railroad yet, but Mara's gaze supplied one, running beside the river and through the middle of the town, its tracks fronted by Mara's invisible corrals and loading pens. There was no telegraph yet, but Mara could look to his left and see a line of diminishing poles. He could even see the tiny birds, like quarter notes, sitting on the wires.

Beside Mara sat Judge Begbie, flamboyantly dressed as always. The two men were seated in wicker chairs, their clean trouser legs stretched out before them. Mara smoked a Jamaican cigar. Begbie drank a glass of lemonade.

"I believe," said the hanging judge, "that many men will essay the tale of this grand empire. But I doubt whether the true story will ever be recited."

"How's that, Scotty?"

The judge squinted his eyes as he looked out onto the sun-wrapped river flats and up at the sudden mountains.

"There are too many different kinds of men hereabouts, who have a special interest in relating their own versions of history. The confounded gun-loving invaders from the south truly believe in their famous manifest destiny. The recent ranchers know almost nothing about the first people who came starving and diseased from over the mountains. The Catholic priests never think of anything less than the entire globe. And there are others, galore."

"There are the Indians and the degenerated products of two races, but they are strangers to history. They have no story."

"Ah, I would not be amazed to find out that they have their stories. But I do know this, that we will encounter great difficulty in telling our story of them," said the judge, waving cigar smoke away from his face.

One late December night we went to karaoke night at the old Riopel Hotel bar in Oliver. It has a different name now, but it still has photos of Windy Bone and his horse on the wall. Most of the music was terrible, bad whitebread, stuffy blood. The best singers were two Indian women from different tables. One sang hot songs from the sixties. The other was twenty years younger and sang hot violent songs from some more recent times. They were both terrific. I mean it. They knew their phrasing and they knew how to belt it out when it needed belting. On the screen where the words to the songs were displayed there were moving pictures of nondescript white women walking around looking sad and comely. My brother went home early. The white moron running the small-town karaoke machine shouted into the microphone. Outside, the thin snow moved horizontally down Main Street.

I keep reading about how important bitterroot is to the Interior Salish people. It is, I read, a somewhat sacred plant, a medicinal food known to the Shuswaps and all the various Okanagan bands. I read that it is the first plant gathered in the spring, that women and their daughters go up the hills and gather bitterroot on a quest that is both sacramental and famine-breaking after the snows and pit-houses of winter.

For a long time I wondered what bitterroot looks like.

One of the important bitterroot places for the Okanagans is White Lake, in the hills south of Penticton. It is above the spot where the falls used to be, just past the southern end of Skaha Lake. It happens that the filmmaker and poet Colin Browne made a movie about the White Lake area. His grandfather was a white pioneer there.

Colin Browne wrote a book of poetry called *Abraham*. It needs a glossary because Colin Browne is an erudite poet, and luckily it has one. There it is explained that bitterroot is also called rock rose. That's what we called it. Rock rose.

If you had your choice between an average red cedar root basket made by a Shuswap person in 1879 and an average oil painting made by a white settler in 1879, which would you go for?

When there is a siege the people on the outside have most of the cards. If there is a card game, the people inside the target begin to despair of reinforcements. If there is a mixing of metaphors, the people inside the little cabin surrounded by frozen ground have little to count on but metaphors. The people outside did not need metaphors. They had the newspapers.

I know there are thousands and thousands, and thousands, most of the people alive in this province of British Columbia, who dont care about young dark-skinned men and boys leaning their heads into the strong wind filled with wet snow, dont give a thought to rabbits puffed up in shallow holes, earth hard as iron. This was actual wide dark land beneath the sharp stars. They spent their short lives, so many of them, blisters on their hands, stinking teeth in their gums, lifting poles, grabbing horses in the cold, slipping in mud in the spring, doors slammed in their faces and behind their backs. Stinking underwear and no soft woman's hands in a million miles. People driving BMWs across Vancouver bridges in the gleam dont give a thought, television colour in their faces at home, where sirens sound from down the boulevard. They never imagine that a teenage boy can lean against a woodpile for warmth that is not there, just a lull in the wind. They dont care at all about a half-breed girl weeping behind a door through which she can hear loud male laughter. I know you cannot make them care. Put a handful of red meat in front of their faces, and they will not know what it is. Lay a waxed rope on the hood of their car, they wont get it. Let a skinny man with brown skin and straight hair step off a curb in their street and they will phone somebody. Put a book on their balcony and they will knock it off, glug a beer, think about buying a pair of boots that will never step on any kind of soil.

I have never been able to understand people who do not have the desire to become famous. I am very much interested in anyone from around my home town who received any degree of fame. But I guess I never thought that anyone from Lawrence or Inkaneep would ever make it out of the valley except into another obscurity. Maybe someone from Penticton would do it. When Ted Bowsfield was brought up to the Red Sox in August of 1958 and beat the Yankees three times, I was glad to be able to remember that he had struck me out with terrifying fastballs seven years earlier. The son of the bank manager in Lawrence made the Gassy Jack statue that tourists take pictures of in Gastown. A boy who went to school with my kid brother is now minister of something in the provincial government. A girl my father once taught in high school was the first woman in the province to get a pilot's licence. Bits and pieces.

The guards were used to fighters and even killers in that cell block. There were a lot of U.S. Americans in the province. There were a lot of Indians who got whisky from the U.S. Americans in exchange for furs and secret stories about valuable stones. There were far more men in the province than there were women. If badly shaven men find themselves in such a country, they have to do something with the whisky in their veins. So they fight.

Sometimes they kill. Sometimes they just bring blood to the surface.

STABBING AT KAMLOOPS—A few days ago
Alexander McKinnon and Joe Walmsby, while
engaged in "manly sports" at Kamloops, quarrelled
about putting a shot, or jumping, or something of
that sort. The altercation waxed warm and reached
the culminating point when Walmsby drew a
jackknife and stabbed his antagonist five times
in the arms and body, inflicting severe but not
necessarily fatal wounds. Walmsby is in jail and
McKinnon is under surgical treatment.

—[*Colonist*]

But the guards did not remember anyone like the
McLeans and Alex Hare. They were not U.S. Americans.
They were not Indians. They were something else that had
come down from the country no one here could imagine.
They were a species. There weren't even any stories about
this kind of person.

"I wonder if there's a lot of them up there," said
one guard.

The two guards were smoking poorly made cigarettes,
under the protection of an eave. It was not raining, and
it was not snowing. Solid wetness was coming down. It
slid on the ground. It slimed the bare branches of a
catalpa tree.

"They look something like Indians," said the
second guard.

"They're no Indians. They're something else."

"They look something like Indians. Except that little one.
He's got light hair. Looks around thirteen."

"He's a killer," said the second guard.

"I seen killers before now."

They stood back as far out of the dreadful falling wet as they could. They pulled out the makings and fumbled and produced two more badly made cigarettes. They leaned their backs against the whitewashed wall.

"Well, people will be taking a good long breath now the Indian uprising isnt going to happen," said the first guard.

"They ought to have a look at these here half-breeds now. People wouldnt worry so much."

"Well, the oldest one."

"Yeah, he'd make me a little nervous, I have to admit. I mean if he wasnt chained to a wall. Even with that hole in his side."

"Can you understand that language they're always talking?"

"Probably Indian."

The wind shifted and sent a gust of mushy wet stuff into their faces. They turned to face the wall until the wind went off another way.

"Another thing I cant understand. If there was going to be an Indian uprising like they say, how come these kids was supposed to be the big troublemakers? How come the Apaches or whatever didnt come swooping down out of the hills? These guys aint Indians."

"Are they white boys?" asked the second guard. He threw his crumbling cigarette into the goo on the ground.

"Hell, no!"

"How many more of them kind you figure they got up there in the country?" asked the second guard.

"I hope to hell there aint too many of them."

"You said it."

"Have to hang the whole works of them, reckon."

The McLean boys were just some half-breed part-time cowboys from upcountry, so who cared all that much? Who cared? Now they were a legal story, and who cared about the legal story? Who cared about the problems in getting the trial going? The government made mistake after mistake, and went ahead with an illegal trial, but who cared?

Still, Confederation was not that old. It was a story a lot of people had not read yet.

They were dangerous boys. But they were locked inside hard rooms. They could see a little grey window on one wall and a rotting door on the other.

My friend Dwight the Shuswap expert was finished his day's work in Kamloops, and it was time to head up Tod Mountain for the night. It was pretty late on a summer's night, and our headlights poked at cutbanks and fences as we wound our way up the mountain road. Dwight was driving ahead, and I was glad for the pretty good pavement on the road. We had been driving up into the night for about three-quarters of an hour, rattling over cattle-guards every few minutes. The car radio was still bringing in late music from the CBC. Here, forty-five minutes from the lights of Kamloops we were in the complete darkness of mountain country, my childhood revisited, but now in smoothly operating foreign automobiles. Dwight had learned to drive only recently, but he knew this mountain ski lodge road better than I did, so I followed, my headlights cutting into the trees as he turned ahead of me. I could see what his headlights illuminated and then I could see the drop away into the canyon of trees that my headlights illuminated before I turned to follow his red tail lights.

Now we were on a short straight climb just before a cattleguard and a quick turn to the right. Between the cattleguard and Dwight's car I saw a figure leap clear across the road and then rise out of the last of Dwight's candle-power, into the roadside blackness. It was a light brown deer, completely soundless, gone back into the trees.

In another ten minutes we were at the ski chalet Dwight was renting for the summer, cool above the July Thompson Valley. We sat on the balcony, our boots on the railing, millions of stars above us. I remembered those stars from my childhood in the Okanagan Valley. We were drinking strong coffee and I was smoking the cigarette I would not allow myself to smoke in my car.

"Do you see a lot of deer on that road?" I asked my old pal.

"See some," he said.

"Phew."

"You see a deer?" he asked me a minute later.

He had been driving a few years. He had told me earlier in the day that he didnt see as well as he would like to while driving at night.

"Uh, Dwight," I said after a few seconds. "I saw a deer jumping across the road in front of you. About the third-last cattleguard."

"That was an eagle," he said. He was sure.

I drank my coffee under the stars.

"Would have scared the shit out of me," he said. "If I'd had time."

Drank my coffee.

"Dwight," I said. "What's the Shuswap word for *eagle*?"

Still the judge on the high *banc* would not be distracted from his solemnity. He kept his hand away from the gavel lying in its pewter tray. The white and black hairs in his crinkly beard hid the perspiration on his cheeks.

"Is it any wonder then that, remaining unchecked and uncared for, they should at last adopt the predatory Arab life, which in a scattered country is fraught with such danger to the state?"

He went on and on, and the jury listened. They had to decide whether these sons of a heroic father were going to be indicted for murder and attempted murder. They listened in the heat and looked from time to time at the forest boys behind the railing.

In the cell block the boys had learned how to yell just loud enough to hear one another. They saved their loudest voices for the visits of warden or guards. Hector McLean was somewhere else now, so his side of the building was made up of eight empty cages.

"What the hell is an Arab life?" asked Charlie.

"Sounds like something they dont like the smell of," yelled Alex Hare. "Called it *predigory*. Sounds like something pretty scary."

As usual in such situations, Allan stayed quiet at first, letting the younger ones thresh it out. He knew they would come to him at last, or leave a hole in the shouted conversation. He let them shout now, after their long silence in the courtroom.

Finally: "Allan, we been living the Arab life?"

"More 'n likely," said Sophie's eldest son.

"Is Arabs some kind of people?"

"The way I think," said Allan, "Arabs must be some people these Scotchmen and Englishmen met up with somewhere they've been taking furs. Good shots. Good horsemen. Must have made a lot of trouble for civilization."

"I'd like to meet some of them Arabs," said Charlie.

"The way I think," said Allan, "those Arabs likely got kind of dark skin."

The lawyers stood the way they always stood. They made all the gestures they were used to. Holding spectacles to eyes while bent to read aloud from a thick volume. Striding tall enough to strain their waistcoat buttons as they used all the frugal space in this little outpost courtroom. Raising an arm on which a cloak hung nicely as they indicated four objects of the Crown's scrutiny.

The jury waited for all this language to finish so that they could get to the hanging.

The witnesses from ranch country were wearing their best outfits. Their hair was slicked back from their foreheads. They said that they knew all about the McLeans and Mister Hare. Some of our breeds are good hard-working individuals, they said, and some just dont know the meaning of property.

The lawyers worked in the blur of history, and they wanted to make this trial as much like a trial in a big city in England as was possible. They were working in a small building beside an icy river that most people would think too far west to picture. But they were in the middle of the place their lives would be given to. Following their deaths they would have streets and lakes and towns named after them.

Look, said the lawyers. The government allows these sons of two races to drift loose, keeps them outside the school and the church, stands idly by while they learn to take other men's horses and cattle and whisky. Then all at once the government changes the rules and sends an armed posse to their mountainside campfire. Who among even our luckily educated youth could respond with cool sanity in such an event? Look, said the lawyers, you have heard from the highest voice in this courtroom that our society is responsible for the error-filled path these lads have taken. We know where true guilt lies.

Listen, said the Crown's lawyer, every act of the prisoners showed that they had entered on a systematic opposition to authority.

The jury waited.

It was an interesting trial. Some day an author should

make a courtroom drama out of it. All the material is there. It will break your heart.

Newspaper readers in Victoria and New Westminster and Kamloops and Toronto loved it. They belonged to a culture of words set in type. They liked to tell stories to their children and neighbours, but words set in type were like words cut into stone. Except that you could hold the newspaper in front of you, open the pages, snap the paper, and commence reading, anywhere you wanted to. Words set in type could lay iron tracks across the mountains. Words set in type could not be mistaken or modified. They were not stories. They were not true stories or legends or family property. Words set in type were the end results of centuries of civilization and serious consideration. They precipitated solid facts out of the fluid of the day's confusions. In parts of this frontier there were flagstones where once there was mud. Words set in type were the flagstones of history. People who could set words in type could go anywhere in the world and make order out of rough country where the unorganized natives had only passed their short lives gathering available berries and slaying unfortunate animals that had wandered into their ambit.

It had been pretty difficult, getting the railroad through the low trees of Northern Ontario. The long backbone of rock had been there all through the life of the planet, and it contained everything the rails contained. But the little men with the rails gouged their way through, foot by foot, yard by yard. Sometimes the earth would turn wet and swallow a working locomotive whole. Trainloads of oatmeal chugged their way westward.

But the mountains of British Columbia demanded sacrifices far greater. They wanted bones, the bones of horses and mules and human beings. A lot of screaming went into the building of the railroad in British Columbia.

Wagonloads of dynamite made their slow and careful

way into the Interior. Men stayed a good distance off and crouched behind boulders. This wonderful explosive soil had been invented less than twenty years before, and even veterans of nitroglycerine were leery of its magic.

But the mountains were made of ancient adamantine. The railroad men drilled rock and placed Nobel's fine soil in the holes. Then they crouched behind boulders. They were learning to be magicians.

A mountain came down piece by piece and fell into the creek. The railroad men filled the creek with angular rocks. From time to time they found seashells in the rock they cracked open.

Goodbye to another creek. Now the red salmon could not believe their information. They did not know where to go.

And the people who had been instructed by their grandparents to come to this spot to find food for everyone could not believe their eyes. There were no salmon. And the next creek was someone else's place.

There were just getting to be too many things to figure out. People could starve to death trying to figure out the things that had been happening ever since the first of these peculiar men had arrived in their black dresses and red beards.

The four young prisoners were wearing hand manacles behind their backs. They were wearing leg irons. These were attached to their boots and their belts, leather and iron. They could stand in the yard, but they could not walk unless they kept their knees locked, their legs stiff. They had to be machines with no intuition.

"They are in the yard," said Moresby. He was very well dressed, in cloth from London.

"You have four men with shotguns, Warden."

"These boys are convicted murderers, mister," said the warden. "They are desperate men."

"Can you remove the wrist decorations, then? I want photographs of boys with arms."

Moresby spoke to the uniformed men with the shotguns. Then he gestured to an assistant, who went behind the Queen's people and removed their handcuffs.

When I was a boy in the Okanagan Valley I looked around a lot. Never knew what I was looking for. Never found arrowheads or ancient Spanish coins in the dust. Found a skeleton once and put the rocks back on top. Found a little pistol once and kept it till it disappeared on me. Found a necklace made of Dutch money. But no one ever told me what to look for. I was scared of McLeans from the rumours I had heard, and I kept an eye out for them. Kenny McLean wasnt in my school any more. I started to wonder whether he was a ghost that came and sat in my classroom for part of a winter.

There was an old woman who lived in a falling-down log house with a framed veranda. It had hollyhocks all around the veranda. A friend of mine told me that this old woman told someone that she once fed Jesse James and gave him a place to sleep overnight. Jesse was supposed to be dead with a bullet in his back, but that was all rigged. Jesse was still alive, and a lot of people knew it. Maybe the law knew it, too, but if Jesse stayed out of bank robbing, they were going to let the legend continue the way it was continuing, Jesse shot in the back while he straightened a picture. When you come to think of it, was Jesse James going to turn his back on a man with a gun and straighten a picture?

So what about the McLeans? When I was a boy I was not told anything about the Okanagan Valley, but I learned a lot about the James gang and the Daltons and the Clantons. All those wild and dangerous brothers from Missouri, where my grandfather had been a boy. But what about the

McLeans? Did they escape? Did Archie McLean escape? Is that a true story about the Kanaka hangman and the severed ropes and the quick horses?

When I was a boy I knew that the James gang and the Daltons were buried deep in history. That was an old old woman who had fed Jesse and given him a bed overnight. But I kept my eyes out for McLeans. I kept my eyes open for McLeans whether they were a gang of gunslingers on the vengeance trail, or peaceful men living out their lives in the hayfields, or ghosts. I did not believe in ghosts, but I believed in God. Still, if there was a God, there was a book about him, and in that book there were a lot of stories about things that can happen even if they are hard to believe. You have to want to believe such things, I had somehow learned.

I still want to believe some things that are hard to believe. There are no gravestones for the wild McLeans. The field where they were buried no longer exists. Who would hang a fifteen-year-old boy?

In the beer parlour in Lawrence, there is a karaoke machine in one corner, but no pool tables any more. Now the tables do not have cigarette-burned terry cloth on them. Now there are framed pictures of famous locals all around the walls. If you look at the pictures, it will not be long until you find a photograph of Windy Bone. Windy Bone is the most famous Indian in Lawrence. I dont know how old he is, but whatever his age is, he doesnt look that old. I have never heard anyone call Windy Bone an elder. If you keep looking at the framed pictures on the walls in the beer parlour, you will keep on finding pictures of Windy.

They try to call it a bar now. They once tried to call it a lounge. Someone once tried to call it a beverage room. It is one of the two beer parlours in Lawrence.

In a lot of the pictures Windy Bone is sitting on a palomino. He is wearing a wide-brimmed hat that casts his face in romantic western shadow under the bright Okanagan sun.

It is afternoon, and Windy Bone is sitting at a table in the cool shade of the beer parlour. He has a glass of beer in front of him, but he isnt drinking it. Windy says he doesnt drink beer any more, but he likes to sit here with a glass. Before they closed the two pool halls in Lawrence, Windy Bone was the best pool shark in town. Bang, the eight ball would be gone, and Windy wasnt even looking when he shot it.

He is wearing his hat, a black Stetson with silver conches making up the band around it. He is wearing strong riding boots that were polished not too long ago. He has a handsome nose and slightly puffed cheeks now. He slouches in his beer chair. If you are not too shy, he will tell you stories. He does not usually tell you the legends you might expect, or the true tales you might expect. Windy has a sense of humour that tells you that you had better be content to be a white man surrounded by irony. A lot of white people in Lawrence say that Windy's a "character." They mean to be comfortable and patronizing. Boy, are they dumb!

Here is Windy Bone's account of the Indian method for catching wild deer:

An Indian rides into deer country, and leaves his horse tethered to a tree. Then he finds himself a nice spot in the shade and waits for a deer to show up. Indians are very silent and patient. When a deer shows up the Indian waits for a while. Lets the deer get over his anxiety and start cropping grass. Then the Indian begins his stalking. He is very quiet and extremely patient, making very small moves, stopping after every move to blend in with the scenery. Once in a while the deer lifts his head with the antlers on it and sniffs the air. But the Indian is blending with the scenery and he is downwind.

It takes a long time, but the Indian is slowly sneaking up on the deer. Now he is just a few steps behind him, blending in. Now comes the hardest part, and this part is what makes an Indian different from a white man. The Indian has to get right up behind the deer without the deer's noticing. Now there is nothing to hide behind.

The Indian makes a careful step and stops. The deer doesnt see him. The Indian is right behind him but the deer is looking in every other direction. Now the Indian is right behind the deer. He can reach out and touch him if he wants to. In one patient and unseen motion the Indian raises his right arm. His first finger is pointing right at the deer. The deer's tail is up. That's the way deer are. In one movement the Indian puts his finger right into the deer's hole. Quick, before the deer can move, the Indian crooks his finger.

Then the deer moves. Well, most people have seen how a deer can move. He can go from standing still and maybe quivering a little, to jumping through the forest in no time flat. You cant see him warming up. He is just gone.

This is where the Indian pays for his deer. The deer is jumping over rocks and under pine trees and between cactuses. The Indian maybe weighs just about as much as the deer, maybe a little less. He's hanging on for dear life, his finger crooked. Every time the deer comes down the Indian comes down, on rocks or cactuses or greasewood. Every time the deer jumps again, the Indian's arm is nearly torn off, and he has to concentrate all his attention on his finger. All his body's strength has to keep that finger crooked. When the deer is coming down the Indian tries to get his feet on the ground, take a few fast steps. But then he's off again.

The deer is hauling somebody that's just about his own

weight. The jumps get shorter and lower. After a while the deer's taking a few steps between the jumps, and the Indian can get on his feet and run for a while. Now the deer is just walking fast. He cant jump any more. Pretty soon he cant walk either. This is when the Indian congratulates the deer for a good run, and then he has him. If he hasnt lost his knife along the way.

"That's the Indian way of deer hunting," says Windy.

"I never knew that."

"There's only one thing to look out for."

"I would have thought there were a lot of things to look out for," says the white man.

"Only one thing to look out for."

"What's that?"

"That deer, if he suddenly decides to take a quick left turn, all you've got is a brown finger," says Windy Bone, looking at the full glass of beer on his table.

When they talked about revenge the priests said that only God was permitted to take a life, and only God was allowed to take vengeance.

"There are other gods with other ideas," said Allan McLean.

"There is no god but the Lord," said Father Chireuse.

"Is this Lord going to get even with Mara for what he did to our sister?"

"There are many Maras and many sisters," said the priest.

The priest sounded as if he had rehearsed wisdom. Allan could not talk that way. He could only sit under a blackened pine tree.

"Will our sisters avenge us?" he asked. He knew what the young priest from France would say.

"Women are the vessels of the Lord's love," said Father Chireuse. He did not know whether the *demi-sauvage* mind could understand the spirituality proposed by human flesh.

Allan looked at the young man in the black skirt for half a minute without speaking, though it was obvious that he would speak. He was wondering whether the priest would know exactly what he was saying.

OTHERS

A Letter from Charles Olson

OLSON AND KEARNS. LIONEL KEARNS was my first poetry buddy, there at UBC, before I met all the guys that made up *Tish*. Years later I was on the phone in Montreal and he was on the phone in Vancouver. I said I'd heard that Olson was ill. "He's dead, man," Kearns said. Some few words you never forget.

Olson was my poetry hero, of course. I should say *our* hero, because though we may have had individual heroes earlier (I, for instance, hankering to be W. C. Williams's son), in the proto-*Tish* days we learned about poetry as a community practice. So Olson.

I was never one for sending letters to heroes. I never thought of working up the nerve to write W. C. Williams. After his death I wrote to Flossie Williams, and got a nice long letter back, from the Virgin Islands. I think I wrote to Olson twice in my life, and got two letters from him—the second contained a hand-written poem for my magazine *Imago*; Olson said that he didnt keep a copy, and would I return the letter. I did. And I had never at that time seen a copying machine.

The first exchange of letters occurred in spring of 1963, a few months before Olson was to attend the famous poetry clambake at UBC that summer. We *Tish* guys were just finishing our suspect M.A.s there. The poem Olson mentions is "Rime of Our Time." I guess I wrote it in early 1963. It first appeared on a CBC radio program called "Wednesday Night," March 27, 1963. It was first in print in *Tamarack Review* 31, Spring 1964, and then was included in my third book, *The Silver Wire*. It seems to be a kind of WCWish poem, and rather neat. I wrote a lot of love poems for Angela in those days, and maybe this one is typical.

As to the Donne poem Olson mentions: I knew it a lot

better then, those ecstatic days, than I do now. When I went to college, I liked Donne a lot. We all had the Penguin Donne, the Penguin Hopkins, and the Penguin García Lorca.

Olson shows here some of that good quick close reading we liked him for, even if we have to disagree, these Pacific ears, sometimes. I did hear the music running through "but" and "us" and the dip into "sounds," all this squeezing out of the sandwich of "scrutinize" and "accumulating." Oh, we rimed and rimed. My personal model in the early sixties was H.D.

I wonder whether my letter exists somewhere. I dont remember whether I was keeping copies of my letters yet. I remember that John Newlove said that we should keep them. I dont remember when I started. If I was keeping copies by then, the carbon of my letter will probably be in the collection at Queen's University. I'm betting against it, though.

But, re my question to Olson. I had never heard of Olson's having a Ph.D. degree, but the brochure for the summer poetry business (UBC was offering credit courses with professors Olson, Duncan, Ginsberg, et cetera) had Olson with a doctorate from Harvard. I had heard that there was an experimental program, and I thought it was called something like "The Study of Man." I think I got that idea from Duncan. Anyway, it is a pleasure to see that thirty years ago Dr. Olson was glad that Harvard called it rather "American Civilization." A contentious phrase for various reasons, but interesting.

I am amused by the last paragraph in Olson's letter. It would have been neat to have a fellow poet and fellow editor named Kah, but here the reference intended is Fred Wah. I dont know why we found that very common B.C. name so difficult. For a year, maybe, I thought Fred spelled his name Waugh. I had no idea that he was part Chinese. Of course that was before he started making a big thing of his Asian heritage just in time to cash in on the recent interest in multi-ethnic activities in the arts. Fred Ka: that would have been even better.

Speaking of the poem Olson mentions, I might mention my first face to face meeting with him. Or rather face to belt buckle. He was coming down a flight of stairs at the Buchanan Building (which would soon thereafter develop cracks in the walls and ceilings) and I was at the bottom of the stairs with Carol Bergé, who was about half Olson's height without the stairs. "Hello," said Olson, "and this must be Angela." In a poem (the first piece in *Curious*, 1973) I made some remark about his not remembering, from the poem I had sent him, that Angela's hair was "yellow." Now thirty years later I have looked at the poem and seen that the colour of her hair is not mentioned at all. Well, Olson didnt always get things right either, did he?

On seeing this letter again (I sold the original years ago to James Lowell) I am mainly, though, struck as countless others must have been, by this major American poet's great generosity to young nobodies. After I heard about his death from Lionel, I drove down to Gloucester and went upstairs at 28 Fort Square and sat on his old wooden kitchen chair and looked out his window at the homely water off the edge of working class Massachusetts.

The letter:

28 Fort Square   Gloucester
Massachusetts
March 7th LXIII

My dear Mr. Bowering,

I like the poem very much. It is very true, & close to beauty. In fact it seems only "sounds" which keeps it short of the latter, and for the life of me I can't see what

else you would have said, having proposed to say
what you do say, after time & the point of the accumulating "sounds."

I think I know what does occur with the word: that
it is, like nothing else in the poem, an occurrence
imagined on a statisgraph. That is, you are both asleep,
and thus comes between the loveliness of your other
statements (as your own senses) such as Angela's hair
on the side of your face, and your two heads—and the
conceptual, that this is "love" and how it is, and (for
me) the "hit" of the poem, that time is now on your
side and *no trick to scrutinize*—lovely. It's ——————

                    here is the key
                    word-wise to a
                    choice which
                    "sounds" isn't

only that "sounds." And there isn't, I'd imagine, anything
more to do about it. That is, this is this poem.

But it caused me to wonder if you know Donne's
poem of sitting by a lady on a bank, and their bodies
touching—knees, I think, is the "contact" (like they
say). At least Donne seems the one who(m), in such
discourse—or at least that "physical" problem you
seem to me to get into with "sounds" (between the two
worlds)—Donne here has been the boldest, and when
"right," looks like Heaven itself.

Anyway, thank you—and I even hear the apposite-
ness of your title, even if at first it seemed large,
and modern.

"behind us days"—& it may be the "but"—yes, I
believe it is: the "but" seems the only lazy moment (again,
to *me*) in the choice of words (that is, doesn't even
"connect" rhyme-wise with anything else?? floats loose??

which is not true of any of the other preposi-
tions (are they?) like the "nice" *or*

OK. Certainly that wasn't your question—but
you "asked" for it! Regards please to Kearns, whom I
enjoyed so much meeting in Toronto a year ago—a
damn pleasure to see him stand out from all the poetry
goons, or poetry "beats"—or for that matter (but these
I never "mind" so much) the "poetry" citizens, the ones
who come out at least to hear a reading—or at least to
look at the traveling monkey. Tell him I talked mostly
to him (as he probably knows) over the "ring" of persons clustering in the sad cleared "dining-room"
(Toronto two-something houses yuk).

Now as to your question: I laughed like hell when
I saw that summer catalogue "Ph.D." (thought it was
Creeley's joke—and fair enough: that is, I sure was
a creature in course long time, and did complete
"requirements" for the same (luckily by studying
Chaucer with Robinson; and the History of the
Westward Movement with Merk (great "Canada"
man: introduced Simpson's fur papers, & taught
himself a most discrete prose to write papers on the
Oregon triangle question: the Master of Pemmican
he ought to be known as when the ages have done
with the present).

But when it came to the degree—and I was
"offered" it one day years later on the steps of Harvard's
library, by Murdoch in Merk's presence—and this will
tell you—for Call Me Ishmael (that is, as the "accept-
able" dissertation—not bad, Harvard *University*)—I
sd, bumptiously and with stupid impossible confi-
dence, no.

So that's the story. With one further fact, to
make the answer complete: the course of study was
not "Man" but—again "credit" Harvard—the first

degrees in "American Civilization," that is the
idea being to take the thing as a unit—law economics
as well as the more obvious culture or "comparative"
businesses—and allow persons to claim some
competence.

It didn't turn out (in the cases of the other two
"original" candidates—John Finch & Daniel Aaron—
you may know the latter's book on the "Progressive"
mind in the U.S.—or now, I see, on "Communism" or
something in the literature of the '30s (or 40s—or
50s)—and it obviously was the first spread of that filthy
virus humanistics (the virus *before* the Asiatic flu cre-
ativity) but there we are: where wld we be if it weren't
that they can now leave us alone?

Best, & please tell Creeley hello (as well for that
matter Davey—*and* Kah (do I have him right?)

Yrs, Charles Olson

The poem:

Rime of Our Time

Here is Angela's
hair on the side of
my face; love as

clean and soft as
it is immediate
to me.   Two heads

on a pillow faces to-
gether eyes closed or
open in the dark.

Time is on our side
now no trick to
scrutinize but behind

us days.   Accumulating
sounds we make in
our sleep, our dreams

of one another seen.

Hello, Down There: Do You Know Who the Canadian Poets Are?

IN EL PASO THE POETS do not generally know who the poets are in Cleveland. They might know that Hart Crane is from there, and some of them might know that D. A. Levy was the main voice of the grimy underground in the sixties. But what about the Cleveland poets? Do they know who the Chattanooga poets are?

In Canada the Winnipeg poets know who the Montreal poets are. The country is five thousand miles long, but the poetry community is made up of people who know each other, and see each other several times a year. This is partly so because many of them belong to the Writers' Union of Canada, and the League of Canadian Poets, and provincial versions of those organizations.

But the main reason is the Canada Council. The Canada Council was begun in the fifties as a bequest from a rich dead person. But now public money is added to the pot in large quantities. It goes to artists and critics of all sorts. Some goes to poetry. The Canada Council awards poets with grants, and sometimes prizes, helps publishers publish poetry and distribute it and publicize it, helps libraries buy it, pays poets for having books in libraries, pays for reading appearances by poets at universities and other places, including Italy and New Zealand, and will even help you print a notice board about news of publications and readings, et cetera.

We Canadian poets are lucky to have the Canada Council.

A couple years before the Canada Council was started, I was just deciding to become a Canadian poet. I did not know there was such a thing. I knew that some friends of mine had a similar idea. One of them, Lionel Kearns, came back from Montreal with a small bundle of books published by new poets' presses such as the Contact Press. There were Canadian poets! More important, they were not dull, not like our politicians and our postage stamps, dull. They were as exciting as the U.S. poets we had been reading, all those young people with their poets' presses, such as Jargon/Corinth.

The first book to be published by Contact Press was called *Cerberus* because it displayed the work of Contact's three editors, Louis Dudek, Raymond Souster, and Irving Layton. It came out in 1950, and would become for young strangers such as myself the signal of the new, the end to the illusion cherished by some elders that our proper influences were Auden and Spender and other Brits who were tilting at windmills we had never seen. In *Cerberus*, the three poets introduced themselves with a few paragraphs of prose. Souster took the opportunity to recommend the poetry of the unknown Charles Olson and to predict that we would be hearing from him.

It made some Canadians in the literature community edgy to hear that the move from fustian to modernity in Canadian poetry was among other things a move from British orientation to American. I was vilified by the nationalistic conservatives and remnant anglophiles back east for aiding the incursion of U.S. poet-thought into our sovereign nation. The attack has been simplistic but unamusing. My U.S. "masters," Olson and Williams, counselled digging deep into your own local condition for your imaginative material. The nationalists in Ontario saw that as a threat to their hegemony over what they perceived as the "regions," a term that denotes something outside Toronto-Ottawa-Montreal.

Poetry, like just about everything else in Canada, is largely a matter of what Toronto calls regions and others call local communities. It is true that Vancouver poets know Kingston poets, but Vancouver poetry is not

Kingston poetry. The history of post-war Canadian poetry is a story of places. Montreal in the forties and early fifties. Vancouver in the sixties. Toronto in the seventies. Winnipeg in the eighties. Calgary in the nineties. Well, sort of. In each case the history was written in new poetry magazines and new poets' presses.

If the U.S. American or Australian reader, say, wants to see what happened in Canadian poetry 1945–1985, that reader would do well to look at the books put out by Contact Press until 1965, by Coach House Press and Talon Books and a few others after 1965. As in the U.S., the news happens in the poets' presses, the "regional" presses, and the very few poetry-hip bookstores.

Here is what has happened in those fifty years: a new poetry that is at least as good as its contemporary south of the border, and better than poetry in English anywhere else in the world. I say this as the imaginary son of WCW and nephew of Denise Levertov and cousin of Ron Silliman.

This is a strange situation. Here we have, just north of the U.S., the best postmodern poetry in the English-speaking world, and most U.S. American readers are unaware of it; and when they become aware of it they cannot buy it anywhere in their own cities. Usually great art follows international power. The Italian renaissance happened when the great merchants of Florence and Venice sent their ships around the world. The nineteenth century saw red spaces all over the map and the greatness of the English novel. Now the U.S. owns and uses and wastes just about everything in the world, and so U.S. culture swamps the world. But now the culture is introduced by bare-chested gun-carrying movie stars rather than literary folk. (In the European universities they know real true U.S. American value—there they study Melville and Poe.)

So U.S. businesses buy our professional book publishers, and book distributors, but we still get the poetry out. Red Deer College Press and Black Moss Books, in places you have never heard of, get the word out—to a few readers and listeners. This is strange. The art in the occupied land is better, perhaps, than the art produced by the imperium. There is a new order. For all the years Robert Kroetsch lived and taught in upstate New York (and co-edited *Boundary 2*), he wrote very good Canadian novels. Since moving back to the Canadian West he has transformed himself into our most admired and imitated poet. Many poets write a good novel or two, and most novelists try to write poetry, but it is very rare that a novelist becomes a very good poet.

Kroetsch is writing or abandoning a lifelong poem called *Field Notes*. Various poets' presses emit the individual sections of it. The Toronto book factories gather it up into a thick product from time to time. In Kroetsch's work one will find the long-anticipated conjunction of the postmodern Olson line and the deconstructive Derrida ex-line. Go back further: the meeting of Ezra Pound and Martin Heidegger. Erase that: the invention of the universe, the necessary base of the great plains upon which can be constructed some marvel that Europe or Ontario never saw but only dreamt, dreamt and repressed. Now we celebrate it. Kroetsch's poetry is a world's fair.

But Kroetsch is just one. Numerous as he is, he is just one.

Before him came Margaret Avison. I am among those who think that Margaret Avison has been the best poet to publish in Canada. But she publishes very little. She was first encountered in an anthology in the late thirties, but her first book was published in 1960 when she was forty-two, and her second, *The Dumbfounding*, was published in 1966 by Norton in New York as a tax dodge. It is a great book. In 1978, 1989, and 1997, Avison published later volumes with an amateur Christian publisher in the Maritimes. But she has written hundreds of unpublished poems, a hidden national treasure, a hope for readers in the future, a belief that our imagination's mortgage will one day be paid off. I wish I were going to be around to see it.

While many approved Canadian poets were showing one another how to make lyrical commentary on life's typical moments, Margaret Avison was looking for the interstices of the divine and the compositional. She became a Christian artist, not just an artist who was Christian. She was writing with calm paradox of a universe but could have meant a lifelong open poem:

> His new creation is
> One, whole, and a
> beginning.

Robert Kroetsch studied and taught in the U.S. Margaret Avison studied at U.S. universities, and was featured in Cid Corman's *Origin*. Raymond Souster published and touted Charles Olson. This sort of thing is still going on. In fact, many of our poets now are U.S. American refugees, from the time of Joe McCarthy through the Indochinese wars to subsequent bombing adventures.

But Canadian poetry is not a branch of U.S. poetry. You will remember that U.S. poetry was once studied as a branch of British poetry. Even T. S. Eliot thought that, and he was from the *middle* West. But U.S. poetry became a great poetry that came to overshadow British poetry. People found out because American foreign policy serves big business and one big business is the book business.

I wish that I could flood the lower forty-eight with Canadian poetry books, but U.S. protectionist laws forbid the importation of more than a few copies of a foreign-published title. Perhaps the more curious and energetic and lucky U.S. readers will get their hands on some of our work and lift it to their neighbourly ears.

Malcolm Lowry on the Beach

I DONT KNOW WHY I DO IT, but I like to visit places where authors lived or died or were buried. David McFadden the travel writer once showed me the grave of Raymond Knister in a cemetery near Lake Erie. I went to the room where John Keats died, and I laid a flower on the grave of Mourning Dove near Omak, Washington.

Malcolm Lowry did not die in Vancouver, though he probably came close a time or two. But he wrote *Under the Volcano* there, or at least a lot of it, just outside the Vancouver city limits. Some people will say that it is the greatest novel ever written in Canada. So a person such as I, who moved to Vancouver just too late to meet Malcolm Lowry (though I met his widow, a former Hollywood starlet, who came in a leopard-skin coat to Earle Birney's creative writhing class), has to deal with ghosts and the sentimental imagination.

I put it off for a long time, but eventually, because I had to write a piece for a German coffee-table magazine, I went for a visit to a turn of Burrard Inlet once called Dollarton, or as Lowry called it in his books, Eridanus.

Burrard Inlet reaches deep between the mountains, past the city of Vancouver, beneath its bridges, turning and dividing and eventually disappearing, a fjord lost in the wilds, a kind of mystery. Across the inlet from Vancouver, and around a point of land just east of the Burrard Indian reserve, is the lost, by now fictional, community of Dollarton. Now there is a quiet green there, called Cates Park, and at the eastern end of the park a forest path called Malcolm Lowry Walk.

Let us say it is a bright day in the middle of December. The temperature is about ten degrees in the late morning, but there is a touch of the night's new snow on the tops of the North Shore mountains above us. Walk along that path, step off it onto the pebbled beach, lean against a smooth boulder, and gaze, as anyone would do, at Phaeton's water. The sun makes the water hard to watch, but the surface looks almost still. The reflected light flashes past you, and when you turn your head you see the glow and shadows playing like a billion fireflies among the bare willows. Like ghosts. From 1939 till 1954, three years before he died, Malcolm Lowry lived here in a succession of shacks on the edge of this water.

Malcolm Lowry was the last great Modernist writer, and the most famous novelist ever to have lived in the Vancouver region. During his years on the beach and his short stays in city apartments he wrote all his major works. Readers around the world associate him with the eccentric Joycean masterpiece *Under the Volcano*, but on the West Coast of Canada, those people who read books love him for his fictions about life here, for the novel *October Ferry to Gabriola*, for instance, and the stories and novellas in *Hear Us O Lord from Heaven Thy Dwelling Place*.

Lowry conceived his life's work, which he was never to finish, in grand terms. Dantean images swarm through the texts, and the *Divine Comedy* is primary among the many structures this ambitious mind was reaching back for. *Under the Volcano*, set in the mean taverns and ravines of Mexico and seen through the suicidal fires of abject alcoholism, is Lowry's Hell text. Paradise was to be in what he thought of as the North, the forest of the North. His protagonist was given the name Sigbjorn Wilderness. Wilderness lives in a shack with his young wife, on the beach at Eridanus.

Eridanus is Dollarton, in the 1940s a collection of shacks on the beach that is today empty on a clear December morning. Eridanus is the god of the river into which Phaeton fell in his fiery chariot, and Lowry has his reasons for thinking of that story. But Eridanus is also the river Po, which reaches the sea at Ravenna, where Dante wrote the *Paradiso*. Lowry wrote in one of his letters that "the celestial scenery of pine trees and mountains, inlet and sea here must be extremely like that in Ravenna, where he [Dante] dies and wrote and got the inspiration for the last part of the *Paradiso*."

But it is a threatened paradise. Across the water, toward Vancouver, the first unnatural thing his eye (and yours) would see is a complex of steel stalagmites on the too-near horizon. This is a major oil refinery, tended by the large tanker ships that invade the cedar-skirted inlet. In Lowry's fiction it is a Shell refinery, and at night its identifying sign glows red in the dark, its initial letter burnt out. Lowry's fictions and his life are filled with coincidences and symbols, as are many people's. If you stood at Dollarton and looked past the Hell sign, you would see the spiky hilltop upon which Simon Fraser University was going to be built. I gave a lot of my years to Simon Fraser University. If you could keep looking in a straight line over the curvature of the earth, you would see from Dollarton, past Hell, past SFU, the ravine into which Lowry's poor dead-drunk consul was pitched, to be found by the hounds of Hell and Mexico.

The great forest is a symbol of paradise, or at least of surcease and hope. One story set in Eridanus, "Gin and Goldenrod," ends this way: "In the cool silvery rainy twilight of the forest a kind of hope began to bloom again." In "The Bravest Boat," Lowry's favourite story, Wilderness and his wife walk through Vancouver's enormous forested Stanley Park, pictured as Adam and Eve in a second Eden.

However, Stanley Park is surrounded by sawmills and oil refineries, man's ugly ego, and by the city of Vancouver, which Lowry reviled. His books are filled with descriptions of the juvenile city as a disgusting place that is neither as innocent as its environment nor as socially graceful as an adult city should be. In one of his most famous poems, he looks at seamy Hastings Street and writes: "And on this scene from all excuse exempt/The mountains gaze in absolute contempt." They saw an ugly sprawl in the middle of stupendously beautiful nature—a city that grew without culture out of its origin as a lumber camp. Sigbjorn Wilderness looks at the sawmills along the waterfront, and sees them "relentlessly smoking and champing like demons, Molochs fed by whole mountainsides of forests that never grew again." This love of the new Eden and horror of the new Babylon is a major theme in British Columbia writing. It was at the centre of Malcolm Lowry's life. It would gobble up mine when I arrived the year he died.

Today at Dollarton, Wilderness's diaphanous hope is still alive. The descendants of the birds his wife tamed are still heard among the alder trees and over the calm water. Occasionally we can hear a light lap of salt water over the pebbles on the shore, even though from around the lighthouse point comes the faint constant drone of some heavy machinery ashore. But Wilderness-Lowry's beloved creek still brings clean water from the mountains, between ferns and wildflowers, over ancient smooth rock, into the sea, still runs beneath Malcolm Lowry Walk into the salt. A hundred metres out on the water, a dog sits in one end of a still canoe, looking at a man in the other end, who holds a fishing pole and sits there, and hopes.

Our Robert Duncan

MANY OF US UP HERE IN Canada wonder why Americans did not have the sense to agree that Robert Duncan was the major U.S. poet after the generation of Pound and Williams and H.D.

A few of us, with that curiosity in mind, consider ourselves very lucky to have been acolytes of Duncan in the late fifties and early sixties. We had seen major poets in our streets in Vancouver—Dylan Thomas, Marianne Moore, Stephen Spender, Kenneth Patchen, let us say. But Duncan arrived among us blessed with a vocation, with a late-Modernist precontemporary religion of poetry. He came as a teacher, unashamedly as a priest of poetry.

He taught us enough lessons to last several lifetimes. First he taught us to read copiously, from the unapproved library, to seek the great forgotten words and bring them alive into our discourse. He taught us that poetry was a cult, not a contest, that all of us in our mutual respect were tending a flame so old that eternity might have been the first fuel. He taught us that we speak our verses with a love for the language that is old enough to be our ancestor. He taught us that poetry was serious, that you give your life for it, that you never use it.

When a bunch of us tyros was considering starting a monthly poetry newsletter, our regular mentor, Warren Tallman, cautioned caution, but Duncan, a guest in Tallman's house, told us to go ahead. What'll we call it, we wondered. Should we call it something like *The Vancouver Poetry Newsletter*? In the doorway between the front hall and the living room at 2527 West 37th Avenue, Duncan said, "Call it *Tish*."

There have been many Canadians writing about Robert Duncan, in and out of universities. In our country there are three generations of poets who write as if Robert Duncan were the great teacher. We hope that the capitals of the United States will learn to regard the books he brought into the world as gifts to the world. To have had such a poet in our midst is to have been more than momentarily blessed.

Three Narratives About
Al Purdy that Explain His Poetry

1

HIS IS THE SADDEST STORY I know. One time the League of Poets was having an annual meeting in Toronto. Here is the way you tell when it was: all the male poets were smoking cigars; all the women poets regarded the cigars as pathetic symbols.

There was a party or reception in someone's big house. The house may have been in Rosedale or some such place. Upstairs bill bissett, assaulted at the time by a bad case of impetigo, was unable to hide from the crowd the fact that he had a big crush on Margaret Atwood. Art Smith was downstairs, smoking cigars with David McFadden, Joe Rosenblatt, Milton Acorn, and me. And Alfred W. Purdy. Purdy was smoking a cigar called a Budgie. You could pick them up at gas station counters at two for fifteen cents. Either that, or he was smoking Trumps. Anyway, Al got a deal buying them by the box.

Al had brought his adorable wife Eurithe's car to the party, something like a 1962 Ford, I think. When it was, for some Ontario reason, time to go, the car was just outside the house, and that was a good thing, because it looked as if Al shouldnt have to go looking for a car this night.

Now, what he had to do was back the car in the half-illuminated darkness, straight to the other end of the long driveway. The driveway was separated from the nearest flower beds by a very low stone wall. Stones with sharp corners. No one could see how he did it, but Al got the right wheels in the flower beds and the left wheels on the drive-way, and drove in reverse, straight as can be, at a medium speed. Sparks flew from under Eurithe's Ford, and there was a loud noise like a hundred Milton Acorns shouting "love." People clapped their hands.

About five books in, Al Purdy arrived at the structure that would characterize his poetry from then on, a non-stop, straight-ahead dash of words, something like one long sentence clearly on its way somewhere, and when it got there so did you. There might be sparks and there might be a grating noise, so if you are not going along for the ride, you'd better stand back and stay out of the way "of something drumming in the blood/of something roaring in the silence/so much like triumph/it sounds like an overture."

All right, it gathers and dashes, gathers and dashes. But you know what I mean.

2

They were the best of times; they were the worst of times, she said. We were visiting at mighty Lake Roblin, my Eurithmic wife Angela and I. It was summer, and the east Ontario deciduous trees were hidden by leaves. Alfred W. Purdy the landsman was showing us around, the A-frame house his wife built while he and the carpenter Acorn were arguing about poetry, the long grass that cooled the ground insects all the way from their front door to the lakeside.

It had been something of a drive from Toronto, especially the finding Ameliasburgh part, and Mrs. Bowering had to go. When you had to go in those days at Roblin Lake, you did not go looking for the kind of gracious bathrooms one might find displayed at a Toronto store called Atwood Interiors. At Roblin Lake the word was exterior, or "outdoor," to put an Anglo-Saxon spin on it. For us guys, the first option was obvious, especially in the hours after sundown. The only question was politeness: how far from the cottage door.

But this was one of those hours of daylight, and Angela B. had to go. Now, she, in those days, had a complex attitude toward Mr. Purdy. She liked his bluff good nature and his endearingly rural sexual innuendoes, but she remained alert enough to keep a step ahead of his pinching finger. Now, however, she had to go, and Mr. Purdy had to show her the uphill path to the outhouse. The next few moments are a blur in my enfeebled memory, but we do have a black-and-white photograph, the kind that doesnt fade with age. The door to the outdoor plumbing is open, and young Mrs. Bowering is seated, her beautiful knees together. A. W. Purdy is holding the door open with one hand, and with his other holding part of a handy shrub before his face. He has one foot on the little crooked board outside the privy, and the other inside, as if he were just stepping out.

In our photo album, Angela labelled this photograph: "Purdy the Faun."

Like a lot of other people in your big poetry anthologies, Al Purdy is a transitional poet. I'm sure he knew that inside himself. He did want to be a transgressor, but he also knew how dear tradition is. Angela got him just right when she called him a faun. Fauns are somehow easier to embrace than satyrs, arent they? And anybody brought up back in our day in Canada learned to love the animals among the trees: "My ambition as I remember and/I always remember was always/to make love vulgarly and immensely/as the vulgar elephant doth/& immense reptiles did/in the open air openly/sweating and grunting together/and going/'BOING BOING BOING'."

As I drove through the wilderness of this world, I often stopped to pick up a friend. A couple years ago, A. W. Purdy and I went to Victoria, British Columbia, to do a reading together at the Victoria Public Library. At last I felt like a fellow old fart. But I did not know anything about this reading date except the time. "What do you know about this reading date," I asked Purdy on the way from his manor beside the ocean north of Victoria. "I was going to ask you the same question," said the slightly older poet. First we had to find the library. Then we had to find the room in which the reading was going to take place. We were getting to be a little browned off. All right, I said to myself, maybe they do treat me better in Bologna than they do in the capital city of the province I have extolled in my writing; but I am here with a living legend, I am here with a national treasure and now a part-time citizen of Vancouver Island. They could at least treat him as if he's something more than the latest Z-generation rimester off the cigarette streets of any spare change.

Not a chance. No one to take us to dinner before the reading. No one to take us for a beer after the reading. No one to show us where anything is. It's a big surprise that an audience found their way there and on the right day. Here's the poets. An hour and a half go by. Time to close up the building. Goodbye. Well, not quite yet: Purdy has a knapsack. It is full of Purdy books. And it is not long until he has a fistful of ten-dollar bills. "You ought to get yourself a knapsack, Bowering," he says, "especially for nights like this."

All right, we are in my car, and for sure there is no post-reading party and no dinner. All we have left is north. Damn it, we decide, we cannot just go to the manor, which Eurithe is not even in, because she is pre-op at a hospital in Victoria. We will turn off the headlights and drive this

Stealth Volvo down Pat Lane's splendid dark tree-lined street. Lane tries to pretend there's no one home, but we keep pounding on his door till he arrives. Eventually he admits that there is a little beer left in the fridge.

This is the first time that Purdy and Lane and Bowering have been alone together, and Mrs. Lane the other poet is back in Ontario being Gzowskied. I love this night. We spend the hours that remain before Purdy's eyelids fall, taking turns telling Canadian-poet gossip stories, and rejoining, "I didnt know that!" I was really surprised at some of the stories Al didnt know. Gee, I wish I could have more nights like that. Three gentle old poets full of gossip and narrative: "what is quietly human and will remain so/when the dancing has ended."

Warren Tallman

The second baseman doesn't think of himself when
he participates in a double play.
—Warren Tallman

TWO DOORS WEST OF OUR PLACE is a house that used often to be inhabited by the best writers in the United States and Canada. West 37th Avenue, Vancouver, B.C. Allen Ginsberg with his alarming beard, speaking speaking speaking in the living room. Charles Olson exhausted, lying on a bed upstairs, speaking. Robert Creeley, elbows on the homemade kitchen table, speaking late into the night. Young acolytes sprawled on the floor because that is all that is left, listening, and best of all, encouraged to speak back, Canadian, full of poetry.

This was the house of Warren and Ellen Tallman, in the late fifties, all through the sixties; it seemed to me to be the nerve centre of anything that was going to happen to verse all our lives. We went there, taking homemade *sake* when we had it, emptying the fridge, scooping hot cookies from the oven, accepting cigarettes and Black Label beer. Ellen and Warren Tallman gave us everything.

We were the young writers of mountain B.C., come to Vancouver hoping for something, never expecting that we would get the best. We were too many to name, because the Tallmans were so bounteous in their gifts and attention. Eventually that little house would be an everywhere, and young poets in Edmonton and Toronto would catch Tallman's attention and come to love this generous man.

Warren Tallman was an angular young man from Tumwater, Washington, a kid with a head full of poetry who would never sleep. He went to college on the GI Bill. He wrote his dissertations on Joseph Conrad and

Henry James, and that should tell you something. These were writers, not authors. They were writers who respected writing and the worlds it could make more than any poor theme. His other great passion was Emily Dickinson, who told a life, "zero at the bone," rather than borrowing from it for material.

Then he met Ellen King of Berkeley, and Ellen knew all the San Francisco poets. First Tallman memorized all their poetry. Then he did what he thought was normal—he began to devote his life to spreading the word, the beautiful word. He became a teacher, an essayist, a convener, the maître d' of contemporary verse. The Tallmans moved to Vancouver in the fifties, and a rumour began in tyro-poetry circles: there was this strange skinny anarcho-muse on the wrong side of the UBC English department. You could sleep on his floor and read his peculiar little poetry books, borrow his car, stay up all night reading your lyrics to him, and get an education such as your creative writing teachers had never got a whiff of.

There were usually at least a dozen people at Warren's house. He would be screwed into the very end of their long couch, his elbows and wrists at angles impossible to most mesomorphs, tracking down some wonderful observation someone had made, looking for the most that living could teach. Somehow he found time to write wonderful essays, always with pencil, always on immense piles of that yellow paper typists used for carbon copies.

When people ask me where I learned to write prose I tell them I learned essay writing from Warren Tallman. He taught me that an essay was what Montaigne knew it to be— writing a life, living a life. He did not have much use for the usual academic essay because he could not find delight in it. He wanted to see that the writer delighted in his work, "sensibility not in its literary but its literal, living sense, life conscious of surrounding life, direct communion."

The writing life, that is.

That's writing as a present participle, as a verb. Warren and Ellen went their separate ways, eventually, and everywhere that Warren lived after that, his apartment was made of the writers he loved. It was as if they were giving something to *him*. Whole walls were made of big photographs of writers. When he organized a season of poetry readings, a thousand people in every audience. He began a poetry newspaper, for heaven's sake. There were signed original poems in frames all over his rooms. Every once in a while there would be a long letter from crosstown Warren in my mailbox, in pencil on yellow paper. He had thought of something, a few words I might have said. In my mailbox there would be a soaring essay, in prose I envied and held to my heart, damn it!

A poet got into trouble with the police; Warren mortgaged his house to make bail. How many literary critics do you know like that? You managed to have a daughter; Warren would show up on her birthday with a perfect present, something he had given careful *thought* to. Living was as important as writing. In the early sixties I was stuck in San Francisco with a couple of Canadian dollars. Warren fixed it so that I had a whole house for myself to live in. A Maybeck house. Tour buses stopped in front of it.

He had a marvellous mind, and taught us western neophytes to respect our own, to take poetry as seriously, to believe literally that we were the children of a mother language.

Here is an accomplishment of his that we did not become fully aware of till late in Warren's life. He memorized the anthology. From Chaucer to Margaret Avison. We thought of him as Mr. Modern, but if you mentioned, say, Sir Philip Sidney, he might recite the whole of "Astrophel and Stella," and in the right accent. Just for that one accomplishment I would give away my Gertrude Stein first editions and half my pension.

Tallman left us two books of essays. They do not begin to amount to his contributions to our writing, but they make for good reading. They are, if we have been paying attention, Warren Tallman.

HAT?

What Is the Grass?

WHEN I WAS IN MY LATE twenties I went to work in Calgary for three years. While I was there I wrote a suite of poems about Alberta, which was published as *Rocky Mountain Foot*. "The Grass" is a small poem that can stand alone (though in reality no poem ever does), or fit properly into place among the other Alberta poems. It is not part of a long poem, but rather a piece in a suite of poems.

It is also, as we later see all poems to be, a poem about making poems. Writing poems might seem to be a pointless thing to do if you have to leave the world in which they can stay. But really, what can you say to the voice that tells you: "Here I am again. Let's go. Get writing!" Grass on the prairie: you've never seen anything so vulnerable, so persistent, so silly and tough.

What can I write poems about? That's what youngsters always say. Look under your feet, said a great American poet over a hundred years ago. Good advice.

$\mathcal{I}$NDEX

Index